BECOMING A *Significant* MAN

BECOMING
A
Significant
MAN

Unleash Your Masculine Self to Become
the Better HUSBAND Your Wife Desires,
Better FATHER Your Children Deserve,
& Better LEADER the World Needs

WARREN PETERSON

New York

BECOMING A *Significant* MAN

Unleash Your Masculine Self to Become the Better HUSBAND Your Wife Desires, Better FATHER Your Children Deserve, & Better LEADER the World Needs

© 2017 **WARREN PETERSON**

Published in New York, New York, by Morgan James Publishing. Morgan James and The Entrepreneurial Publisher are trademarks of Morgan James, LLC. www.MorganJamesPublishing.com

The Morgan James Speakers Group can bring authors to your live event. For more information or to book an event visit The Morgan James Speakers Group at www.TheMorganJamesSpeakersGroup.com.

Shelfie

A **free** eBook edition is available with the purchase of this print book.

CLEARLY PRINT YOUR NAME ABOVE IN UPPER CASE

Instructions to claim your free eBook edition:
1. Download the Shelfie app for Android or iOS
2. Write your name in **UPPER CASE** above
3. Use the Shelfie app to submit a photo
4. Download your eBook to any device

ISBN 978-1-68350-123-7 paperback
ISBN 978-1-68350-124-4 eBook
ISBN 978-1-68350-125-1 hardcover
Library of Congress Control Number:
2016909318

Cover Design by:
Rachel Lopez
www.r2cdesign.com

Interior Design by:
Bonnie Bushman
The Whole Caboodle Graphic Design

In an effort to support local communities, raise awareness and funds, Morgan James Publishing donates a percentage of all book sales for the life of each book to Habitat for Humanity Peninsula and Greater Williamsburg.

Get involved today! Visit
www.MorganJamesBuilds.com

TABLE OF CONTENTS

PREFACE

A few quick notes about this book, before you get started:

This book is for men, from a man's viewpoint. I know that many women have read and enjoyed these chapters and learned plenty from them, and if you're a woman I hope you do as well. All I ask is that you keep in mind that this is from a man's perspective. If your man is going through his evolution to becoming more, please be patient, understanding, and supportive in his desire to be more, and please be sure to examine the chapter titled, "She Stood Up".

This book is for men who are married, or plan to be; men who have children, or plan to; men who are entrepreneurial, or plan to be; and men who have questions about faith and God. If you're the kind of man who already has his Bible memorized and who can let everyone else know what they are doing that is wrong, then you'll likely not enjoy this book as much as a man who isn't in the same place as you.

This book is a series of short chapters, so that you can quickly read one or two and get back to your life with some new ideas to think about and some new questions to consider as you go through your day. I've heard from many men that they end up reading the entire book in one sitting, and then re–read it again slowly, highlighting and underlining the important parts they want to keep revisiting, when they go through it again.

I wrote this book in a personal and conversational style, as if you and I were sitting down and having a conversation together. If you're interested in a scripture–filled or research–styled book about men and masculinity, please realize this isn't the book you're looking for.

I wrote this book with lots of questions posed to the reader. When you see the questions, which kick–off right away in the first chapter, take the time to think about them. You should consider opening a notebook and writing down your answers. Don't just read past the questions like any other sentence, the questions are there by design, to make you think—so take the opportunity to really do that.

This book includes generalities about men, about relationships, and about life. That is the only way to discuss such large subjects as this in short chapters. There will always be exceptions to every rule.

Importantly, there is no one definition of significance for every man, nor any singular fixed description of a significant man that applies to every man, so if you feel that parts of this book don't apply directly to your life, then they most likely don't!

Lastly, this book is not the end of your journey it is the beginning. If you are interested in going deeper and you are seeking to walk the walk with other men who are seeking to become more then please do check out what we have going on over at www.SignificantMan.com

ACKNOWLEDGEMENTS

This book is the result of a lifetime of learning, leading, connecting, and growing that continues to this day. Thank you to all the friends, family, teachers, coaches, and mentors that I've had over the years.

Most importantly, this book would not exist without my amazing and beautiful wife Carin. Thank you for your patience and putting up with me as I brought this book to life and for being the greatest supporter of my work with Significant Man. I love you and I am forever yours.

To my incredible children Janna, Danielle, Grace, and Benjamin, you continue to teach me something new every single day. I am grateful and proud to be your father. I love you.

To my mother and father, Wayne and Marie thank you for the love, the prayers, and the sacrifice that you have extended towards me over the years. To Paul and Mary, thank you for welcoming me into your family with grace and open arms.

To my sisters Susan and AnneMarie, and to my brother Brett, thank you for always being there with your support, your encouragement, and your wisdom.

To David Hancock, this book would only be an idea if it wasn't for you and your entire team at Morgan James Publishing. Thank you for being the best publishing team on the planet!

To Kelly Johnson, thanks for your keen eye, for catching all my typos, and for putting up with too many commas and my crazy style of writing.

To the powerful men I have shared my walk with over the years: Waleed Aldryaan, Bill Bowron, Ken Brown, Steve Crabb, Darryl Johnson, Scott Kepner, Gene Longobardi, Matthew Nimeth, Mark Patrick, Bryan Pierson, Steve Richter, Brian Schulenberg, David Young, and Robert Young.

To the great leaders and men I have met more recently along my journey; I appreciate the examples you set and the insights you share. I have learned from you directly and indirectly, and continue to every day: Joel Comm, Setema Gali Jr., Eric Graham, Brian G. Johnson, Kevin Knebl, Ken McArthur, Ryan Michler, Kevin Nations, Christopher John Stubbs, and Sean Whalen.

To the many authors I've learned from over the years; your work continues to influence me to this day. My path would not be clear without the road you laid in front of me. Thank you to Robert Bly, Gordon Dalbey, John Eldgredge, CS Lewis, Dennis Prager, Dennis Rainey, Stu Weber, and many more.

To the many remarkable women I have met, online and offline, thank you for your encouragement and support: Lezlie Brown, Theresa Byrne, Shelley Hitz, Debra Jason, Lise Lansue, Tracy Malone, Melissa Nations, Zsuzsa Novak, Jessika Phillips, Tracy Richter, Felicia Slattery, Tina Spriggs, Michelle Van Otten, and so many more.

INTRODUCTION

The average man today is sleepwalking through life; without ever reaching his potential and without ever crossing the line to living a more significant life. However, it goes deeper than simply needing to wake up and live.

Yes, men need to wake up. Yes, men need to step into their power and reclaim what they have given away. Yes, men need own their current reality; own the state of their life, their finances, their careers, and their relationships, all of it. Men absolutely have to wake up to this truth.

As you continue past this truth you start to realize that men have to wake up because when they do not they are doing far more damage than simply staying asleep.

These men are dying.

Men who are passively letting their lives slip past them, men who are simply drifting along in their lives, going in whichever direction the water takes them, these are men who are beyond bored. They are dying.

When I walk down the street today and look into the eyes of men, I see man after man who is sleepwalking, man after man who has given up on himself, simply waiting for each day to end.

These men look for all sorts of ways to disengage with life, ways not to wake up. They remain asleep, most men actually not wanting to wake up. These men get lost in watching sports, playing video games, binge watching television, working harder and longer hours, or they bury themselves in their drinks and their drugs, anything to keep themselves from waking up.

That is killing men; their sleepwalking is actually a slow suicide.

Too many men are disengaged, not caring about anything or anyone, other than the surface level platitudes and unremarkable statements they squeak out in order to avoid conflict.

Too many men are disconnected from themselves and from God, no longer even interested in searching out the big answers to the big questions they asked earlier in their lives.

When you see these men, you see men who have lost that look of life in their eyes, there is no sparkle, there is no energy, and there is no enthusiasm. They are dying.

When you see these men, you see men who have no ambition for anything other than playing a new game or watching a new show, you see men who have no mission or vision for their life. They are dying.

When you see these men, you see men who look at their own lives with detachment; they look passively back as if they are looking through the window at a stranger, not at themselves. They are dying.

When you see these men, you see men who have all the stuff that a successful man is supposed to have, but you see men who have emptiness behind their masks of success. They are dying.

If you are one of these men, you have to wake up. Your sleeping is not just passing time; it is killing you. If you are one of these men, you have to choose another path. Your complacency is killing you.

You have this power in you already; you have this ability right now. It might be somewhat daunting to think about taking your power seriously and to think about becoming fully awake, but this is required.

You have to wake up in order for you to become the significant man that you know you have inside.

As you read along you will learn that for far too long men have been hiding; hiding from their wives, their children, their communities, and from themselves.

Men have been walking through this life feeling alone, feeling like all they have to offer is to focus on earning money, as if the paycheck alone will give them value, purpose, and enough to survive on.

As the famous line, from one of my favorite movies states:

"Wake up, Neo… the Matrix has you."

It's time for you to wake up. It's time to realize that you have given away your power while you have been sleeping. No, you likely didn't do that on purposes, in fact you likely didn't even realize it was happening.

Once you have realized this, once you know of this new reality, it is time to open your eyes to what is in front of you, and to the life you can live. You can choose to step out of hiding; you can choose to wake up, and to step into the power that you have buried within.

You have incredible power, ready to unleash on the world. However, in order for you to get there, you have to honestly want to. You have to choose to stop with the distractions and stop with putting obstacles in your own way. You have the power; it's time to use it.

It's time for you to expect more. It's time for you to stop falling back into the old patterns that have been holding you back for your entire life.

If you've ever said, or thought, anything like this, then you need this book:

"I know that I have so much more inside, so much more to offer this world, and so much more to give."

"I want to become the hero, the warrior, and the leader that I was created to be."

"I can't stand not knowing my kids, or them not knowing me."

"I can't stand my wife turning into my roommate."

"I can't stand this feeling of being alone and not sure where to go next with my life."

"I know that I have more to me than my success, more than my money and my stuff, I am ready to move from seeking success towards living a life of significance."

"I want more. I want to experience more. I want to understand more. I want to have an intimate relationship with my wife. I want to lead my children.

I want to connect with God. I want to learn more. To know more. To do more. To BE more."

If those are the things you know you want deep down, but you're still working up to saying so, then this book is for you.

If you think you already have everything you want, if you think you already have everything figured out, if you think you already have it all, then this book isn't for you.

If you're open to new ideas, to new challenges, and new ways of thinking, then this book is for you.

If you're sure your ways are already good enough, and you don't like to be pushed to think about new ideas, then this book isn't for you.

I wrote this book as the result of my own journey and to honor all the men I've worked with over the years. The simple fact is that men, all over this world, are seeking more, but feel like they have no outlet and no place to turn to. To make matters even more confusing, our society has thrown all the rules out the window, has discarded universal truths about men that have grounded us since the dawn of time, and as a result men are confused and are struggling.

No more.

This book is the start of a journey, not the end, and it is a journey that I am honored to be on with you.

Your life isn't about the man you are today. Your life isn't about the man you were in your past. Your life is about the man you are becoming. No matter where you are right now, you can become more significant, you can become more connected with God, you can become the father your children deserve, you can become the husband your wife desires, you can become that man…

…and you can choose to begin right now.

So, let's get started.

Warren

Founder, Significant Man

http://www.SignificantMan.com/

One

THE MEASURE OF A MAN

The questions that haunt most men may sound simple to many, but to us men who are seeking more out of life we know these are anything but simple questions.

Are we really men? Are we doing what men are supposed to be doing? Are we living the lives we were created to live? Is this all there is to life?

In other words, and what those questions are really asking is, how do we measure ourselves as men?

For the majority of men, the answers come down to our stuff; so we measure ourselves by the cars we drive, the homes we live in, the vacations we take, and the toys we buy for our family, our friends, and ourselves.

This is an easy way for us to measure ourselves, because each of these things, all this stuff, is very easy to see and identify. You can visually see the difference between a Ferrari and a Ford. You can visually see the difference between a mansion and a shack. All men can see these differences, and this makes for an easy and quick way to measure success.

However, measuring ourselves by our things leaves a hollow feeling inside, and never really answers those haunting questions we have deep down inside. Measuring by things simply confuses the situation.

This is why so many successful men are burnt out, hurting inside, numbing themselves to the reality of this life. They are in pain, but don't know why. They are seeking fulfillment, but doing so in ways that will never fill the hole they have in their souls.

Not only are those ways not filling the hole they each have, but those ways are actually making the hole bigger, cutting deeper, and opening a canyon sized feeling of emptiness and pain they can't quite describe.

The stuff cannot fill that hole; the toys cannot heal the pain.

As we continue, I want to extend this to another interesting question for you to think about.

Watch any two men meet each other for the first time. Within a few seconds of the initial handshake and hello comes the question, "So what do you do?"

To men, this is not a simple question (and to the ladies reading along, this might be a revelation for you). In reality this question is the start of the measuring between the two men, it is asking who in the conversation has done better, who should be listened to, who will be more respected, who the winner is, and it is asking who is more successful with life itself.

That's why so many men dislike that question so much, even if they have never actually thought about to this depth before. Because that one question is how most men measure themselves and the other men they meet. Usually this isn't intentional, it's just that men don't have any other tools or questions to use for this measurement.

Which then raises the obvious follow–up; since that is so hollow, and since the stuff never really works and leaves men empty inside, how should a man measure himself? How do you measure your success as a man?

Let's think about another way to look at this critical question, in a way that is perhaps quite different from how the world and our society tends to measure a man.

This new idea about how you can measure yourself as a man might take some time for you to really grasp, but this is incredibly powerful for you on your journey towards becoming the man you know you can be:

A significant man can be measured by the overall emotional and spiritual health of himself personally, AND the overall emotional and spiritual health of his family.

In more detail: a significant man is a man who has a vision and direction for his life, who creates an intimate relationship with his wife, who builds up and leads his sons and daughters, who connects with God, and who will powerfully defend all of that when the trials and challenges come to tear it all down.

Without this, without the vision and without the leadership, his family will be hurting, his family will struggle, his family will have a dark cloud hanging over all decisions, and his family can become lost in the wilderness of life. If he and his family do not have emotional and spiritual health, no matter how much money he has, or how many things and toys he owns, or how much he has bought for others, he will never feel at peace as a man.

Take a step back today and consider those two points. How is your own emotional health and that of your family? How is your own spiritual health and that of your family?

You might have all the toys, own a successful business or great job with the corner office, and take vacations to exotic places around the world, but if your emotional and spiritual health are not well, the truth is that you are not living the life of a significant man. If you think you have that health yourself, but your wife and children do not, then again you are not living the life of a significant man.

It is time for you to reconsider how you measure yourself as a man. It's not about the toys, it's not about the gifts, it's not about the stuff. It is much deeper than that, it's actually on a whole other level that most men never reach.

When you get to that level, when you start to see life this way, and when you start to measure yourself as a man this way, then you know you have taken a great leap forward on your journey towards becoming a more significant man.

Two

THE POWER OF YOUR CHOICES

When I'm working with men one thing I am constantly talking about is the power of choice, which is related to why I ask so many questions.

Sometimes, especially with someone who is new to the idea of taking control and living a significant life, I'm asked if the concept of choice itself is really that important, or if we can simply "float through life".

Considering that this is a theme of mine, choices in life, and is something that comes up in so many conversations, I want to expand on this concept of choice right away.

Almost everything you have in front of you today, both the good and the bad, the positive and the negative, it is there because of a choice you have made in the past.

If you're reading this in print or electronically, that was a choice. If you're reading this in your home or away, that was a choice.

The car you drive, the house you live in, these all were choices you made. The clothes you are wearing today, the work you do for a living, these all were, and are, direct results of the choices you made, and continue to make.

4

Where you went to college was a choice. Where you got your first job was a choice. The subjects you studied in school, or the work you decided to do last decade or last year, were all choices. Those early choices all led to new choices as you moved through life.

The woman you would marry. The church you would attend. The children you would raise. All choices.

Your fitness and health level. Your financial situation. The legacy you are building. All choices.

You may look back and wish you had other options to choose from, or you may look back and think that you wish you had made different choices, but those are different conversations. Even in the choices you regret, you had options and you played a role.

Often I hear men tell me that their life isn't a result of their choices, they feel that other people have made choices for them, that other people have been in control of what has taken place, and that they really had no input on what was decided.

The hard reality is that that is almost never the case. The reality is that you were part of those choices; you were not a powerless bystander. Those decisions that you didn't like, you did have the option to say No and you did have the option to go a different way.

It might have been harder, at least at the time, if you had said No or if you had made a different choice. That's true. It might have cost you financially or it might have cost you a relationship, but there was a choice to make, and you made it.

Please note that this is referring to adults, not children. Decisions your parents made for you, when you were a child, are obviously a separate issue. This concept is about the average everyday man, dealing with everyday life.

At some point you have to accept the truth that the life you have, right now, is a result of all the choices you have made, both good and bad, over the course of your entire life.

Owning this truth is hard for many, it forces a serious look in the mirror and acceptance of the truth. It is not easy; which is why it is not something most men will choose to face.

Most men don't want the truth, most would rather run from the truth, or pretend that somehow this doesn't apply to them. Most men will find an excuse, find someone else to blame, find some reason to be a victim, and most men will create some reason not to accept this reality.

However, if you are going to live the life of a significant man you do accept this reality and you don't run from this truth. In fact, not only do you avoid running from this truth, instead you run headfirst towards it.

The reason you run towards this truth is because you realize the power it holds. You begin to become aware of the choices you have made, the ones you continue to make today, and the ones you will make tomorrow, and then realize you can use that truth to your advantage.

This is a critical step in living a life that you design. A life that provides you with what you desire, and a life you control. Because when you realize that your current situation and your past situation were all built upon the results of your choices… that means that your future is also built upon the results of your choices, and that is a powerful realization.

Your future tomorrow is a result of the choices that you make today. There is serious power in that awareness.

Realize that now you get to make those choices with this new awareness and understanding. Now you get to be strategic, you get to build and plan your life based on this truth.

Now you get to think about what you want next year to look like and you get to decide what you have to do differently to make that happen. Now you get to look at every decision in front of you and you get to decide which choice will move you closer to the life you are seeking, and which choice will move you farther away from that life.

When you're getting ready to make a choice, if you don't have a clear answer, if there isn't an obvious choice that will bring you closer to the life you want to live, then pause. Wait. You can take your time to decide.

Step back and really think about the options, think about what moves you to where you want to be.

Realize that you have incredible power through the choices you are about to make.

You get to choose your future.
What will it look like?

Three

MOST MEN WON'T DO THIS

T his is one of those painful truths that I wish wasn't so. But here it is: Most men won't live the life of a Significant Man. Most men won't be willing to go deep, won't be willing to ask themselves the tough questions, won't be willing to open up, won't be willing to dig into their wounds, won't be willing to invest in themselves, won't be willing to make the changes, and most men won't be willing to do the work.

Most simply won't.

Oh you'll hear many who talk the talk. You'll hear many who say they want it. You'll hear many who make it look like they are interested in experiencing those changes on the outside, but when it comes down to making the change, when they are standing on the line and have to make a decision, most men will choose to remain where they are.

I get it, I understand. For the longest time I said I wanted that life, I said I wanted to become that sort of man, but I really wasn't fully committed and wasn't ready to actually cross the line to the other side. I was not going all in. I wasn't willing to invest in myself. I wasn't willing to do the hard work, and to confront the hard realities of my life.

You see we all get comfortable, and that state of comfort is both a blessing and a curse. Because change is different, it is new, and it is unfamiliar. As humans, we tend to really love what is familiar over what is different, even when we're pretty sure that different place/thing/life is where we are supposed to live.

For years, I was the guy on the sidelines, the guy who knew I was called to do more. I knew that God put me on this Earth to do more than earn a paycheck. I knew that God did not put me here to sit in an office cube month after month. I knew that God put me here on this Earth to really help people, to impact lives, to change generations.

But I waited. I hesitated.

I needed the time to be "right".

In hindsight, that waiting only cost me one thing: time. I wasted years waiting for the right time. I had excuse after excuse as to why I wasn't ready, why I couldn't take the risk, why I couldn't invest in myself, why I wasn't able to do what God created me to do.

The reality was simple. I was more comfortable with the familiar place I was, even though it was the wrong place for me to be, than I was willing to change and become the man I was created to be. No matter how tough and bad things were, they were still familiar.

When I was there (and if you've been there or are there, you know this too), the annoying voice in my mind kept making those excuses louder and louder. My inner self was doing all it could to keep me where I was, and it was very easy to find justification for staying there.

Staying there was just so much easier than really investing in myself and making the changes I needed to make in order to improve my life.

This is why I understand these challenges so much, because I lived that, I knew it first–hand.

This is why I don't judge any man who chooses to remain small and stay safe where he is, as I did when I didn't realize any of this. We all make our choices in our own time, and we all live with the consequences of our choices.

It does make me sad though to know so many men are sitting on the sidelines, so many men are wasting away, so many men are numb to life—unaware of what they could be experiencing and living today.

I know what could be for them. I know what life can be like.

Imagine you are the world's best swimmer (which I am not!) and you see someone in the pool, working so hard to swim to the other side, barely staying afloat. You know how much easier it can be, you know how they can switch from working so hard to letting their body naturally move through the water, you know how much they could be enjoying their experience... yet they struggle, because they have chosen to do so.

That is quite often how I feel, to be honest. I see men who are choosing to struggle. I see men who are choosing to do nothing other than talk, men who go home and don't lead or even really talk with their kids, men who go home and are not intimate with their wives, men who do not have any understanding of or connection with God.

The truth is that for most men they will be content with such a life, living small and safe, living in the protected, comfortable, and familiar reality they have created for themselves.

If you're reading this however, I have different expectations for you. Yes, I have expectations for you, even if you are "only" a reader of this book.

I expect that you want more out of life. I expect that you are willing to open wounds and ask serious questions. I expect you to wake up. I expect that you will not settle and remain numbed to life.

Most importantly, I expect that YOU expect more for yourself. You expect a better relationship with your wife. You expect to lead your family and children. You expect to connect with God. You expect these things.

Because you do have these expectations, and because you have cracked open that door and peeked through to the other side, I expect that you will do whatever you have to do in order to become the significant man that you were created to be.

Four

NO ONE ELSE

*I*t isn't my job to save you.

Despite the great words that men share with me, about our work together, and despite how much I do appreciate such kind words, it isn't me. Period. I make that very clear.

Yes, you need men to walk with you. Yes, you need men who have your back, without judgment. Yes, you need leaders, mentors, teachers, and coaches who are willing to own their part of the process, their part of your journey in becoming a significant man. However, not one of them is here to save you and none of them can do your work for you.

In fact, no one, not one single soul on this planet, no one else but you, can do your work.

I can help you, I can lead, I can teach, I can mentor, I can show new realities, new opportunities, and I can show you what life can be like. (And, if not me, there are many other mentors and teachers for you to find.) However, at the end of the day, you are the one who has to do the work. You are the one who has to take what you learn and put it into practice.

If you have had an argument with your wife, no one else is coming there to have the conversation with her. As difficult as that conversation might be, you are the only one who can have that talk.

If you have disconnected with your kids, no one else is coming to rebuild that connection. As challenging as that re–connection might be, you are the only one who can build that back up.

No one else can force you to grow. No one else can make you change.

No one else can take your responsibility. No one else can take your power to decide.

No one else can step into your place and do what you have to do. Even with all the tools, advice, practice, support, and anything else you learn, you ultimately are the one who is implementing the solution to your problem.

You can ignore this, as many men sadly do, for as long as you are willing to put up with the results of you thinking someone else will come to save you. In other words, if you're ok with the results you get from putting this onto someone else, then you can go on ignoring this for as long as you like.

You can pretend that it is about finding a savior, as so many others do. You can pretend that there will be a savior to come and rescue you at home. You can pretend that there will be a savior to come and rescue you at work. You can pretend that there will be a savior that will come and rescue you in your finances or in your health, but deep down in your gut you know that isn't going to happen.

Important side note: I'm a Christian man of deep faith, and I'm not talking about Jesus as Savior or the concept of Salvation here. In this chapter, I'm talking about you, your responsibilities, and getting your own work done.

This is where so many become stuck, as they are waiting for someone else or something else to show up and do their work for them. They are waiting for a magic solution, an easy button, or a secret product that will allow them to skip forward to the benefits, without actually doing the work, and they remain stuck because of that.

If that's you, just know that the longer you wait, the more that you put the work off, the more that you think it is up to someone else, the longer that those painful parts of your daily life will continue. As long as you are holding out, maybe with the hope that your wife will go first, that is exactly how long you will be waiting, hurting, and knowing that you need to do the work.

When a man tells me that he has been waiting, it hurts, it really does. I know he can make a different choice and stop waiting. I know he can choose to go first and start to have that difficult conversation that has been building over time, and that is becoming heavier and heavier to carry.

I never promise that these things are easy, I never suggest that there are some magic words he can simply say that will somehow make everything ok (that would be looking for the savior "language" to show up for him, so that he doesn't have to do it himself).

Can we talk about specific strategies he can use? Absolutely. Will I give him suggestions and ideas that he can use? Absolutely. At the end of the day however, he is the one who will have to do the work, he is the one who will have to talk the talk.

The same is true for you. You are the one who has to decide you want more. You are the one who gets to build a passionate relationship with your wife. You are the one who gets to create a powerful connection with your kids.

There is no one else coming to do your work for you. There is no one else coming who will be able to walk in your shoes for you. There is no one else coming who will be able to take your voice and have your conversations for you.

You get to do all of that. You get to do the work, no one else. You.

When you do, you also get to enjoy the rewards of doing the work. You get to experience the pride of doing what you know so few other men ever will. You get to experience the new life you have created. You get to sit back and reap what you have sown.

It's up to you. Are you ready to accept that?

Five

WHO DO YOU HAVE TO BECOME?

As you sit there reading this today, I want you to think about your life. Seriously take some time and think about where you are now; think about where you thought you would be by now, and think about where you think you are honestly heading right now.

How are your finances today? How is your health and fitness today? How is your relationship with your wife and with your children today? How is your faith today? And where are those headed, specifically and exactly where are you headed in each of those areas?

We all have goals, we all have ideas, and we all have dreams we want to turn into reality.

But most men never do make their dreams come true, as I mentioned in a prior chapter, Most Men Won't Do This. Most men never cross the line from living a life of average to living a life of significance. Most men never escape the trap of chasing after success.

What about you? Where are you right now, today? Are you where you thought you would be?

Is your life what you thought it would be? Are you living the way you expected you would live?

If you're like me, and like most of the men I've spoken with, there was a time that you sat back and thought about these issues. That led you to look at the life you had and to asking one fundamental question:

Is this all there is?

This is a point that almost all men get to, at some time in their lives, and interestingly this isn't impacted by financial wealth. In other words, men who are at the very top and men who are at the very bottom both ask that exact same question.

Very wealthy men and very poor men both ask, "Is this all there is?"

There is a drive deep in the souls of many men; a need to create, to build, and to change the world, and these are incredibly powerful needs.

For me, I knew I had so much more inside. More to give, more to offer, more people to serve, and more to create. I knew that I was here on Earth to impact generations. Like so many other men, I was born with the "Earth–changer" gene.

It doesn't matter if you have that gene or not, I'm willing to bet you have asked that same question. I'm confident that at some point you have wondered if the way your life is now is the way it is going to be for the rest of the time you have here on Earth.

So that question, "Is this all there is?" is powerful and will start you on the journey of where you can go in life, but that one question is only the starting point to get you to the next place.

That next place is the important second question. A question you have to be willing to ask yourself, and you have to be willing to hear the answer. That question is:

"Who do I have to become?"

Once you start wondering "Is this all there is?", and when you decide that you want more, it is very important that you continue on and face this next question. Because you do have a choice, you can either ask, "Is this all there is?" and become depressed at the answers you create for yourself, or you can be willing to consider the second question.

Clearly, the man you are today, the knowledge you have right now, the skills you have at this moment, those were enough to get you to where you are, but those are not going to be enough to get you to where you want to be.

If the knowledge and skills you have today were enough, you would have already used them to be where you want to be. If you already knew enough, if you already had the systems in place, you would already be there. As great as your background is, and if you're the kind of man who is reading this you do have that background already, you know that you need to keep pushing forward to gain new insights and new skills.

Visualize and think about your life when you have reached that place which you consider significant. Think about what your relationships will be like, think about what your financial situation will be like, think about what your health and fitness will be like, think about what your faith will be like, and think about what your friendships and business connections will be like.

To push this even further, what will your wife think about and say about you when you have reached that place? What will your children think about and say about you when you are there? Really figure out what they would say, how will they describe you and your relationship with them at that time?

Once you have that image in your mind, once you can see that future, then ask yourself:

Who do I have to become in order to get there? What do I have to learn in order to become that man? What new skills do I have to acquire? What new knowledge do I have to get? What investments do I have to make? What other changes will I have to make?

What this means is that you will need to be open to the reality that who you are today will not be the same person as who you will be when you've made the changes you have to make. You will have to become more. You will have to leave the old you behind and be ready to go deep on those questions.

Because not only are these excellent questions, not only are these great things for you to consider, but these are actually the required questions that drive men to more significant lives. These are the questions that those same driven men keep coming back to, keep thinking about, and keep considering, until they are comfortable with the process of finding the answers.

You want that significant life? You want to live a life that is beyond the "Is this all there is?" life that you are living today? You want to become that man you have visualized?

Awesome! So in order to do that, who do you have to become?

Six

YOUR BLIND SPOTS

O ne of the single greatest advantages of choosing to work with someone else, as you take the journey towards living the life of a significant man, is to have a perspective from outside yourself.

It's hard for most men, maybe even for all men, at least when first learning and appreciating how much this is a powerful benefit and advantage, to be open to input from others.

Especially men, since we're supposed to be able to figure everything out for ourselves (yeah, right… we all know how well that has worked out so far!), have a resistance to getting this input.

One of the most important benefits to you joining up with other men who are also on the same journey as you are on is this: the perspective into your blind spots.

As you know from driving, blind spots are serious. Blind spots are where you're cruising down the highway and something dangerous, maybe even life threatening, happens, and you had no idea that danger even existed.

Imagine you have your family in the car with you, driving on the Interstate, when you start changing lanes. You hear a horn and, at the last second, you pull the steering wheel to get back into your lane. You nearly caused a horrific accident, involving your wife and kids and another family in their vehicle, all because you didn't see what was in your blind spot.

Just like when you are driving, you have blind spots in your life as well. You have blind spots in your relationships, in your business, in your goals, in your connection to God, and on and on...

Think about it like this:

On one hand, there are challenges you know you have, and you're working on them. That's a good thing, and those are not your blind spots, because you know about them.

You might know that you need to lose weight, so you get to work on that challenge. You might know you need to earn more income, so you get to work on that challenge. You might know that you need to become a better father, so you get to work on that challenge.

You create plans for those challenges, you get input on creating even better plans, you get a fitness coach to help you along, and so on. Those are all good for you to work on, but they are not involving any blind spots.

On the other hand, there are challenges you have in your life right now, and you don't even know they exist. Those challenges are the ones that are hiding in your blind spots. Those can be the most dangerous of all challenges, but to you they are invisible, and so you're blind to them.

Just as when you're driving some of the worst accidents can happen due to what is in your blind spots the same is true in your life.

Because you can't see them, and in order for you to avoid the coming danger, you need someone to spot those challenges for you.

The sorts of blind spots we have in our lives can quickly run deep into big issues. We might have blind spots tied into our values, our beliefs, our thoughts, our ideas, our actions, and so on.

As an example. I once worked with a man who called his wife, "the wife" as a nickname, which is actually quite common. I asked him about that, asked if he knew, or had ever asked, what his wife thought of that nickname. Some wives are fine with that nickname; others are not, while others are indifferent.

He said he never once thought about it, he never thought about asking her; it wasn't something he ever considered. That is a perfect example of a blind spot in life. It is something others can see but we can't.

I suggested that he go ahead and ask his wife about that nickname. It turned out that she really disliked it, it made her feel like an object, and that she wished he never used it. This took him entirely by surprise, because it was in his blind spot, he never saw the danger that was lurking there.

You need someone you can trust who will shine a spotlight on your blind spots, in a positive and productive way. It doesn't really help to have someone simply point out something they say might be bad and move on. You need actual strategies and suggestions to work with.

Uncovering your blind spots is something you should consider a primary requirement in your journey towards living the life of a significant man.

As a great side effect of learning this process, the more you discover and find your blind spots, the quicker they are to address. You'll start to develop a better awareness of yourself, and will move faster towards that life you're now designing. You'll start to become more open and receptive to uncovering your blind spots.

Since this idea, getting someone to work with you uncovering blind spots, is new to most men, keep in mind that your blind spots don't always equate to something that is negative. Is it common that they are negative? To be honest, yes probably so. But not always, and the end result is positive—avoiding the car wreck is a good thing!

Finding a blind spot becomes a great way to recognize that you're growing. When you find them, and then when you do something about them, you can take comfort knowing that you have learned something and are changing something right now that will have a positive impact on the rest of your life.

If you're wondering, yes the blind spots can get smaller over time. The more you are looking for them, and the more the guys who have your back will seek them for you, the smaller they can become. Keep in mind though, that they never really go 100% away, there will always be some blind spots in your life, because your life keeps changing. Over time, you become more flexible and faster at reacting to the news, and you realize that these are positive changes for both you and all those who know you.

While it might not be very fun at first to have your blind spots shown to you, being able to react and adapt quickly is a skill you'll be able to use and teach other people your whole life.

So let someone else check your blind spots for you, and then get back to cruising down the road.

Seven

THE WOMAN AND THE NICE GUY

We'll call him Joe, but he could just as easily be you or me.

Joe was a nice guy and he was a good guy. He was always willing to help others, there was always a smile on his face... he was the guy who would say yes when you needed someone to come and help you move into a new house.

Joe would give you a ride when your car was in the shop. Joe would agree to go to the movie you wanted to see, even if it was one he didn't want to see.

Joe was a nice guy, and he never saw it coming.

One day, a day Joe thought was another in a long line of him being a nice guy, his wife left him.

Joe was in shock, he was devastated, but somewhere in the back of his mind, he was not surprised.

He sat there, numb, as she walked past him, her bags already packed.

She looked at him, willing him to say something, wanting him to do something... but he just sat there dumbfounded, seemingly without a clue.

So out she walked, she left.

He had no idea what just happened, and no idea why. He knew she was a great woman, he knew she had ambition; she had goals, dreams and desires. He did his best to say yes to her, to give her what he thought she wanted, and to make sure that their house was one of peace without conflict.

Later, he found a page from her journal, which she clearly left behind for him to read.

"I wish Joe would just, I don't know, get angry sometimes. Not like angry and violent towards me, I don't mean that, I just mean be willing to have a fight for what he wants and what he believes in. I can't recall the last time he said something that he wanted. I don't even think he really wants me anymore. He sure doesn't seem like he is willing to fight for me. I love him so much, I really do, but I can't live with a man who isn't willing to fight for me."

Guys, this story is all too real in the world of today. Far too many men have laid down their sword, laid down their shield, and stopped fighting. They have stopped fighting for anything really, going numb to the world and sleepwalking through life.

In the modern world of today, women don't need men to go out and fight off the attackers in the literal sense, but women do need men who are willing to fight for them.

Your wife wants you to fight for her, to fight for your future together, to fight for what matters most in your life.

Far too often, the nice guy is unwilling to fight; he is unwilling to go to those places. He is unwilling to rock the boat, unaware of the damage that he is bringing onto himself and his relationship by being so unwilling to go there.

Joe was afraid of getting angry or of anything that might not be "yes". Joe was afraid that if he let that part of him out, that if he was anything other than accommodating or pleasant, that she would leave him.

He learned the hard way that what he was doing would be part of the reason why she did walk out the door that day. He learned that somewhere inside, he had lost a part of what made him a man to begin with and had started to lose part of his own identity.

He was so concerned with being nice, so worried about upsetting anyone and anything that he ended up losing that which was most precious to him.

Consider the following from author Robert Bly,

"In The Odyssey, Hermes instructs Odysseus, when he is approaching a kind of matriarchal figure, that he is to lift and show Circe, his sword.

It is difficult today for many of the younger males to distinguish between showing the sword and hurting someone... They learned so well not to hurt anyone that they can't lift the sword, even to catch the light of the sun on it!

Showing a sword doesn't mean fighting; there's something joyful in it."

I would argue that this quote is now true for all males, it is no longer limited to younger males, as written.

Showing your sword isn't about hurting people, that is never the goal. It is about being willing to stand up and speak the truth, even if you know it might create challenges for you.

Your words and your actions are your Circe, they are your swords, when was the last time that you actually wielded them?

Don't end up like Joe. So withdrawn back into his "nice life" that he became unaware of what his wife actually needed from him.

Be willing to be "less nice". Be willing to go into the arena, get dirty, and fight.

Let her see the passion, the power, and the persistence you have that you are not going to lie down, you are not going to let life happen to you. Let her see that you are willing to risk what you have, for her. Let her know that you will not stop fighting, for your family, for her, and for yourself.

Let her see you lift your sword and catch the sunlight gleaming off the blade.

Eight

SO YOU WANT MORE SEX?

You probably want more sex, don't you?

Most married men will answer yes when asked if they want more sex, more fun and more passion in the bedroom. That question is up there with, "Do you want to breathe?" for most men: Yes!

Most married men will also answer with frustration that they have no idea what or how to do anything differently, in order to get back to those nights of fun and passion.

I've heard many men complain that women just don't get it, that they don't understand how important sex really is to men.

You know what? That's absolutely true, the vast majority of wives have no idea what sex means to their husbands, what the frequency of sex means, what that sexual connection really means for their man. That is completely true, and is completely for another audience at another time.

Yes, for you ladies reading along, you do need to understand your man better, and if you want him to become the man you know he can become, then understanding his sexual nature is a critical point for you. He really does need you to want him sexually. Now back to the guys...

So what are you to do, how can you do anything that will help get back to the nights of passion in your bedroom?

I need to back up first. First, you need to understand this isn't about "getting" your woman, or tricking her into sex, none of that junk you see all over online. I absolutely cannot stand the Pick Up Artist scene, I think that is a disgusting disservice to men and women alike and wish all that stuff would just disappear.

This chapter is about you and your wife, the woman you love and adore. It is about that connection. Just like wives need to understand their husbands better, you as the husband in this conversation, need to understand your wife better and understand what drives her.

One of her biggest drivers is trust. I've heard from many women that "without trust there is no lust", so think about that for a minute. While it does sound like a fun and simple line, it is also a line overflowing with truth. Trust is that big of a deal to her, trust is that important to her.

You need to realize that while us guys can, and often do, compartmentalize sex, that doesn't tend to happen with women on the same level. You need to realize that distrust out of the bedroom directly leads to distrust in the bedroom, she directly connects those two issues.

In fact, for your wife nearly everything that happens outside the bedroom has an impact on what happens inside the bedroom, which is odd to us guys, since that isn't the case for us, at all. However right now, I'm focusing on the singular issue of trust and how that influences what goes on inside your bedroom.

Let me ask you this, what things are you doing to earn, and to keep earning her trust, and what things are you doing to break her trust?

Have you made commitments to her, which you have not kept? From big things to little things, all of them matter, even the ones you forgot entirely!

Have you lied to her, openly or covertly? Are you keeping things from her? Even if she doesn't know the exact details, her amazing feminine intuition knows that something isn't right.

Have you avoided conversations with her? Refer to The Woman and The Nice Guy chapter above to revisit how this can snowball into something major.

Have you avoided conflict, by withholding serious thoughts and feelings you have? This is also related to the Nice Guy; don't withhold from her. She is smart enough to know something is going on anyway.

Is your behavior towards her, and around her, clear and focused? Or are you "wishy washy" and unclear about what you want? Yep, Nice Guy again. Seeing how big of a deal this really is yet?

Don't assume that the trust is always there, you need to keep working to earn it. Even if you haven't done anything to break her trust, if you take it as one of your jobs as a man to keep earning her trust that is only a positive thing for your entire relationship (which directly leads to positive things in your bedroom!).

Give yourself the job of becoming more trustworthy, in every area of your relationship. Let her into a little corner of your life, where no one has ever been before, and tell her that you are entrusting her alone with that information.

Your mission, if you choose to accept it, is to become the man that she can trust, with every aspect of her life. Become the man that she knows, in her soul, will hold firm to honor her, and that you will be the rock of trust that she can always rest her weary self on.

Does this take time? Of course, all great things take time. You know that. You're on a journey to become a significant man, you're not on a journey to flame out fast.

If you're feeling brave enough, show her this chapter, and even the prior one The Woman and The Nice Guy. Ask her for her opinion, then be quiet and listen to her. See if she agrees that, "without trust there is no lust".

I sure hope you do accept this mission; you might be surprised by how something from outside your bedroom heats things up inside your bedroom.

Nine
YOU ARE AT WAR

You are at war; you are in the midst of the battle of your life, a battle for your very soul as a man. You are fighting for who you are as a man, you are fighting to become more, and your enemy is out to make sure you do not win.

You might not even be aware this battle is going on; you might not even realize that you are at war. Your enemy hopes it stays that way; your enemy doesn't want you to even know this fight is underway.

After all, if you aren't aware that this battle is taking place, how can you possibly win? How can you win a fight you aren't even aware that you're in?

The simple answer is that you can't. Until you realize that you are in the middle of this fight, you can't win.

Your enemy has clear and specific goals. Your enemy is out to crush your spirit, to suck the life out of you and to make you retreat into the shadows. Your enemy wants you to be a small, hollow, and empty man, a broken shell of who you could really be.

If your enemy gets his way, you will never become a significant man. You will never fulfill your potential. You will never have a great relationship with your wife. You will never have the financial wealth you deserve. You will never

28

experience the abundance the world has to offer. You will never be the leader of your children. You will never run a great business. And you will absolutely never have a connection with God.

Your enemy uses the most effective weapon, in the history of the world, to accomplish his goals.

What is that weapon, you might wonder? What is this most effective weapon, the one that he will use to keep you from becoming the man you were created to be?

It is your own mind. Your enemy uses your own mind against you, and against everyone you are called to lead. Your mind is where your doubts, fears, insecurities, and questions, all grow and fester; often until they are paralyzing.

Think about this quote, from author John Owen:

"However strong a castle may be, if a treacherous party resides inside (ready to betray at the first opportunity possible), the castle cannot be kept safe from the enemy. Traitors occupy our own hearts, ready to side with every temptation and to surrender to them all."

Imagine that you are the castle John is talking about, that your life itself is the strong castle.

You might have the strongest body of anyone you know, you might have the largest bank account of anyone you know, but in your mind is where your enemy attacks. Your enemy weaves the thoughts into your mind so deeply that you think they are your own thoughts. Your enemy put those traitorous thoughts into your heart, and then he attacks.

One result of this attack is that you soon find yourself pulling back on conversations where you are no longer willing to share your wisdom or thoughts. Here is an example of what I mean by this idea:

Too many men, maybe even you, have been hurt in the past when sharing your opinions and observations. This leads you to longer speak up unless you are confident that your thoughts will be taken well; you don't want to make a move unless you know ahead of time that your action is going to lead to success. You have talked yourself out of sharing, without the guarantee of success.

That's no way to win, in fact you can't win that way. Your enemy loves that. Your enemy is thrilled that you have pulled back into the safety of yourself, that you no longer risk upsetting someone. And this is just one tiny example of how this battle is fought all day long.

When you choose to pull back, you lose, and your enemy wins.

When you choose not to take advantage of an opportunity, when you choose to play small, you lose, and your enemy wins.

Do you want to move forward in life? Then take the risk of saying what you want, of voicing your opinions, of sharing the wisdom that you have to offer. Take the risk of investing in yourself and doing something different from what you have ever done before, something that is for you.

What have you been holding inside? What have you wanted to share with the world, but you have talked yourself out of? What have you wanted to engage in, participate in, or rejoice in, but you stay on the sidelines due to concern over how other will perceive your actions?

Challenge yourself to have one conversation today that you have been keeping inside. It doesn't need to be the biggest thing you are thinking of, but have some conversation that you have been talking yourself out of. When you do, keep in mind that this is you being on offense, this is you deciding that you are no longer going to sit on the sidelines of your own war.

Then repeat this, and have another conversation the next day. Every day have one conversation that you've been holding onto.

This battle for your mind is taking place, maybe even right now as you read this. One part of you sees this happening in your life and that you should change, and the other part is telling you that you can't possibly do this or have the conversation you're thinking of.

You know it is already happening, your very soul is in the middle of the battle. Now it is time to accept this reality, so you can take off your blindfold and get into the fight.

Arm yourself with the truth, grab your sword, put on your helmet, hold your shield, and face the enemy.

You will win, but you have to fight. It all starts with you realizing that this battle is taking place, this very minute.

Now get into the arena, and fight.

Ten

WHAT ARE YOU WAITING FOR?

When I ask this question to the men I work with I'm met with an amazing range of answers. It is a simple sounding question: What are you waiting for?

If the question sounds so straightforward, why is it that the answer seems so hard to find? Why is it that men struggle with such a "simple" question?

- You want to make more money? OK, so what are you waiting for?
- You want an intimate relationship with your wife? OK, so what are you waiting for?
- You want to lead your children? OK, so what are you waiting for?
- You want to connect with God? OK, so what are you waiting for?
- You want to invest in yourself? OK, so what are you waiting for?
- You want to become the Hero, the Warrior, and the Leader that God created you to be? OK, so what are you waiting for?

Most men, probably including you, can come up with a whole range of answers to these questions. We can all easily come up with a list of reasons why we have to be waiting right now. We can all easily come up with a list of reasons why the time isn't right, and why it probably won't be for a while.

The reality is that those answers, those reasons you have been defending with such energy, they are actually a list of excuses. If you read the prior chapter, The Battle Of Your Life, you know that those excuses are all part of your enemy's plan to keep you from reaching your goals and becoming the man you know you can be.

Somewhere deep down in your mind you already know this to be true. You know that they are really excuses, but you might not be ready to confront that reality. This issue right here, becoming aware that your reasons are just excuses, is a major milestone that you can be looking for. You will know where you are, on your journey to becoming the significant man you know you have inside, when you are open to accepting this truth.

You see, the average man, the average guy you see all day long, he is not ready to face this truth. He will defend his excuses, often with extreme passion and intensity. He still gives his power away to his excuses, he lets those reasons dictate his future, instead of him being in control and not allowing those excuses rule over his life. He is happy to share all the reasons he has to be waiting right now, and he can quickly give you the list of excuses when asked.

The significant man, on the other hand, is aware that those reasons are really excuses. Instead of giving those excuses power, he starves them. He faces them and works to make sure they do not become the rulers over his life. He knows the excuses are part of the battle he is fighting, and since he is on offense, he is going to make sure that those excuses have no power over him.

If the significant man wants to invest in himself, he finds a way instead of finding excuses. If he wants to lead his children, he learns how and starts leading them. If he wants an intimate relationship with his wife, he swallows his ego, and he takes the steps to create that relationship. If he wants to connect with God, he opens his heart to that connection and allows himself to listen and learn. If he wants to create a larger income, he is open and willing to learn new ideas, concepts, and strategies he can put into action.

Instead of giving the power to his excuses, he gives the power to himself. I want you to think about that before moving on. There is power and energy in every situation, if you're holding onto your excuses, then you have transferred the power that is rightfully yours away to your excuses and suddenly those excuses seem to be holding power over you.

It is time you take that power back.

Notice that nowhere am I suggesting this is easy, and this point is true for most of this book. To walk this walk takes effort. You have to be willing to do the work. You have to be willing to get hurt in the process, which is very hard for most men.

Learning something new can hurt. Just like when you go through a new workout, your muscles will be sore from working in new ways. That hurt is a good hurt though, it is evidence that you are growing, that your body is adjusting, and that you are on the right path.

The same thing is true in your mind and in your soul. Men who are on this journey will be working out their minds and their souls, and they will accept that hurt is part of the process.

It all comes back to the question, what are you waiting for? Are you going to continue to accept those answers, are you going to continue to give power to your excuses?

Or, are you going to face the truth that you can retake the power to start now, that you have the choice to make today the beginning of the next steps on your journey, and that you will no longer wait?

The time is right now, today. You can't afford to wait anymore to make the changes you need to make. Don't allow yourself to fall back on the same excuses you used in the past, make a commitment to yourself that your change starts today. You can become that man, and you can start right now.

Eleven

THE FATHER WOUND

I ask that you hang in there for this chapter, as this one might be challenging. This is not a long chapter, but isn't an easy subject. You know by now that this book isn't just empty filler and simple feel–good stuff, but is instead real insights you can use in your life. This one might be tough for many.

OK, here we go…

Most men have a very painful wound in their souls that came from their fathers. This is different from the more often discussed mother's wound (in our society when someone has a challenge we hear the stereotype of "tell me about your mother"), which can also be a painful wound, but that is a separate topic for another book. The reason that the father's wound is different is because the father's wound is often buried deeper, so much deeper.

The father wound comes in both subtle and in obvious ways, both of which tear into the very foundation of a man.

One of the main reasons that so many men feel like they are walking around as a fraud, and not really as a man, is due to this father wound. When this wound goes undetected and unhealed, it affects the man's entire life, from his finances to his health, from his relationships to his faith, from his attitude to his expectations of life itself. It is that big of a deal.

Below are some of the common statements I've heard from men, about their fathers, over the years, and I'll bet these are not all that unfamiliar:

- Nothing was ever good enough for him.
- He never once said I love you.
- He never approved of my decisions or me.
- He bought stuff for me, but was never there for me.
- He never shared anything real with me.
- He told me I was weak.
- He said I was a Momma's Boy.
- He said I would never amount to anything.
- He was always silent; he knew nothing about me.
- He cared more for his hobbies and toys than me.
- He always said I should do better, be better.
- He would mock my career choice.
- He would question my ability as a husband and a father.
- He would compare me to him—and I was never good enough.
- I could never live up to his expectations.
- I never really knew my father.
- And on and on…

Does any of that sound familiar? If so, you are in good company. I've heard all those from men over the years, and I could keep going with that list for pages.

Please note I'm not talking about bad fathers or bad men here. I'm not talking about men who are physically abusive, who constantly berate their children. Those challenges have their own unique needs, which must be addressed by qualified professionals. That's not what this book is about. Here we are talking about the average ordinary good man.

Most men want to be good fathers, in fact most men want to become the best fathers they can, most do not want to cause any wounds to their children, most want to protect their children.

However, it's a surprise to no one that men are imperfect, and since most boys will mirror their own fathers when they become fathers themselves, the cycle is repeated and the legacy of the wound will live on for another generation.

That wound, the father wound, is at the heart of everything. It becomes life defining; it becomes part of who the man is. Sometimes the wound becomes the man's very identity.

Men must heal this wound in order to move along on the journey of becoming a significant man. Men must come to terms with this wound, must be willing to acknowledge that it exists, and be open to healing it. If not, if the man insists there is no wound, insists everything is great, insists that he has it all together, then growing past this point is not possible. The likely outcome of his denial is for the wound to continue on harming the man and then continue for at least another generation in his own children.

The understanding that this wound exists is step one. For some it is easy to identify, there was a big outburst, there was a tragic event, or there was a clear and obvious wound. For others, and this is majority of men who grew up with good men who were trying hard as fathers, the wound is not as obvious, and it takes time to uncover.

You must go down this road, you must find the wound in your life, and then you must be willing to have the courage to walk straight into the wound.

It hurts. It is not easy. You have to go there however; otherwise, you will still be seeking the answer to this wound when you are on your deathbed…

PS—This is a subject that is many books by itself; I can't go to serious depth in a short chapter like this. My goals here are for you to start to think about this, to think back about the origin of the wound in your life, and to see if you can identify how the father wound might be showing up and affecting your own life and the lives of your wife and children.

Twelve

REAL MEN DON'T GET DEPRESSION

You know it's true, because you've heard it your whole life:

- Real men suck it up.
- Real men just walk it off.
- Real men rub some dirt on it.
- Real men don't know it when they are bleeding.
- Real men are stone statues moved by no one, by no event, and by no person.

And, without question, real men don't get depressed.

Right? After all, if that is what we've heard our whole lives it must be true right?

Well no, it isn't true. It's time to get rid of this horrible family–destroying and life–destroying lie. Real men certainly can, and do, get depressed and deal with depression.

Depression is serious, and is unfortunately misunderstood by most. Depression can, especially in men, truly be life–threatening, so no this is not something to just rub some dirt on, and then keep going with your day. Depression is not something to ignore or pretend doesn't exist in men.

Since men historically don't ask for help on these issues, nor even talk about these issues, dealing with depression in men can become even more complex to work through. Even many researchers in this field openly admit to not diagnosing male depression the same as female depression, in part due to this historical truth about men.

Because men keep their depression inside, versus openly talking about it, we all need to be on the lookout for the signs of depression in men. While all men and women who experience depression share some common symptoms or signs, there are some signs that tend to be more evident in men, and they look like this:

- Burying himself into work
- Becoming more easily stressed
- Having increased levels of anger
- Taking thoughtless serious risks
- Choosing not to have sex
- Increasing drinking or drug use
- Increasing physical pain everywhere
- Increasing illnesses
- Thinking he is no longer a real man
- Thinking about suicide
- Overwhelming feeling of discouragement

Men, here is the truth: everyone, EVERYONE can experience depression. It is not a sign of weakness. It is not a sign of being less of a man. It is not a sign of failure.

It is a sign that you are human. The end. Period.

Us guys need to all stop buying into the lie that real men don't get depressed. We don't need to put on the mask that everything is ok, looking the part on the outside, all while walking around with this depression and darkness on the inside that's eating us apart.

When you break your leg, you get help for your leg and move on with life. It would be beyond silly to tell a man with a shattered femur to simply rub some dirt on it and walk it off. The same thing is true with depression. When you get depression, you get help and then you move on with your life.

Getting help is exactly how you demonstrate to your wife, your kids, and all those around you that you are a real man. Being willing to take off the mask is the way you show everyone, most importantly yourself, that you are not playing the game, and that you are ready to start climbing out of the darkness.

I've been there guys; I've dealt with depression. I understand the darkness, the pain of hitting rock bottom, and the sheer amount of effort it takes just to get out of bed and get moving. I know that place all too well.

It is not a place where men (of course women as well, but I'm talking to the guys here) ever want to be. And so I'm aware of how misunderstood depression really is. Unfortunately, in our culture we have the phrase, "I'm feeling depressed" which makes it seem like "depression" is just a bit farther down the scale from "I'm feeling depressed", when they are actually two different things entirely. If I had a magic wand, I would create an entirely new word or phrase to separate those two concepts.

The simple reality is that men do get depression, and it is very serious. Men are taking their own lives, every single day, because of depression. The suicide rates in men are many times higher than they are in women (if the statistics were reversed, this would be front-page news), and that is in part because men internalize all that is going on in their lives so much.

It is time for you, for me, for all of us, to discard this myth and to allow both ourselves and our society to walk alongside men through their challenging times.

If you happen to be there now, just know that it isn't forever, that you aren't going to be down there in the darkness forever, even if it feels like that is the case today.

Always remember that no matter where you are right now, "This Too Shall Pass".

Thirteen

AN EMOTIONAL MAN

I'm starting this chapter with a quote. This is from David Smith, the author of *The Friendless American Male*:

"Very early in life, little boys receive the cultural message that they're not supposed to show emotions. Expressing feelings is generally a taboo for males.

Boys soon learn to dread words like: Don't be a sissy. Big boys don't cry. Aren't you a little too old to be sitting on your daddy's lap?

Other messages come through loud and clear—boys have to learn to be men. And to be a man means you conceal your emotions."

This quote is powerful, and goes to the heart of a serious issue for men, which is concealing and showing emotions. Beyond that, there is the tendency to think that men should not only be concealing their emotions, but that they shouldn't even have them in the first place.

If you read much of modern culture, it says that men aren't emotional and that they are only logical. While it is absolutely true that research shows the male brain tends to function more on logic than the female brain, research does not show that men are not emotional people (just like research does not show that women are not logical people).

Additionally, the modern culture often says that men shouldn't be emotional in the first place. Despite the lip service given to this subject, the "real man" shown in the media is still the bearded interesting man who shows little to no emotion, other than maybe while he is shooting something or blowing something up. While at the same exact time, the culture is saying men should change to be both more emotional, be more in touch with their feminine side, and repress their masculine side. The fact that men are confused on this subject shouldn't be a surprise to anyone.

A good part of this confusion came in times that are more recent; think the silent and stoic John Wayne as an example. It is an odd change, to be honest. If you think back throughout history, many of the great men and great leaders who changed the world were very emotional:

- In the bible, David was a powerful warrior, a feared King, and he was emotional.
- In American history, reading the letters written by George Washington shows he was emotional.
- In ancient world history, Plato and Aristotle worked on theories of powerful emotions.
- In the famous Hollywood movie, *Braveheart*, William Wallace showed his emotion all throughout the movie. Braveheart would not be who he was without his emotions.

When you study these men, you soon realize that it is actually hard to be a great and significant leader and not be emotional at the same time.

Part of what drove those men to significance was the fact that they did have emotions and that they were emotional. The people around them saw the emotions, and knew that they were powerful men, the sort of men that others wish to follow.

Who would you rather follow into battle? A leader who was always cold and showed no emotion, even when one of your brothers goes down, or a leader who shows that he cares deeply about every man who is shoulder to shoulder with him on the same mission?

The answers seem so obvious, yet still, we hear about all the men who are unwilling to allow their emotions to exist on the outside, and we still teach that men shouldn't even have emotions existing on the inside. We still see the man who wants to be the unmovable man made of stone.

Some men have been so conditioned on this issue, that even when they are at the funeral of someone they loved, they won't allow themselves to cry. Even later, in the privacy of their own home, they may stop themselves from crying.

Guys, it is ok to cry at a funeral, it is ok to let the pain out, to go through the stages of grief. That is ok!

If this idea of being an emotional man is totally foreign to you that's ok too. For many men, this is the result of a culture that has spent a few generations trying to get men to believe, do, and act in a way that is counter to how they were created in the first place. For many other men, this is directly a part of the father wound discussed in the earlier chapter.

If a man was raised in a home where "real men don't cry", this will take longer. Again, that's ok.

We have to learn to move from holding everything inside and we need to learn to be ok with who God made us to be, which is both logical and emotional. In addition, we need to drop the constant "I'm fine" thing.

Ask the average guy on the street how he is doing and his answer will be, "I'm fine." Ask the average guy you know how he is doing, and his answer will be, "I'm fine."

Before I dug deep and went down my own journey towards becoming a significant man, if you were to ask me how I was doing my answer would have been, "I'm fine."

I bet this is the same for you. It doesn't matter who asks you, it could be a total stranger, it could be your best friend, it could be your wife, odds are that your answer will usually be the same as mine was, "I'm good." or "I'm fine."

But you know, and I know, that is almost never the truth. That is almost never how you are actually doing. That is almost never how you are actually feeling.

If you're at all like me, you know that in reality the answer to that question is more like this: I'm sad. I'm excited. I'm lonely. I'm thrilled. I'm confused. I'm in the zone. I'm hurting. I'm happy.

In other words, most days there is something going on inside, and you want it to come out, but you feel the pressure of the culture saying that you aren't supposed to have these thoughts and emotions.

So we end up doing what men have done for generations, we put those emotions and feelings inside a box, lock it up, and don't let them out. We believe the myth that we will be more respected, more appreciated, more loved, and be perceived to be more of a man if we keep that box locked up tight and don't let our emotions out.

We believe the lie that emotions equal weakness. We believe that by even mentioning our emotions, even granting them any light of day, we are somehow going to be discovered as less of a man, and so we won't take that risk.

Now here is where we flip this whole thing upside down… here is the truth.

The truth is that in your emotions you have tremendous power. Yes, power. Those emotions are not weakness, it's just the opposite: they are powerful. Remember King David, William Wallace, George Washington? Yes, powerful is a word that goes along with each of them.

This is because your emotions contain truth, and truth is powerful. When you hide your emotions, you are lying to yourself and those around you. Lying is the other side of power; it is a draining and negative force.

When you live more and more in the world of truth, you experience situations with a completely new perspective and with a completely different kind of power.

Imagine going through your life without having to cover up your emotions anymore. (Note: this doesn't mean you have no control over your emotions or that you are no longer logical in your life). Imagine being able to answer people honestly and truthfully when they ask you how you're doing.

This idea is so foreign to most men that there is immediate resistance to the idea. Let's do a quick and basic test. How do you answer this: Do you think you could do through your entire day tomorrow being honest about your emotions and honestly answering when someone, including a friend or your wife, asks you how you're doing? Could you do it?

For most men, the idea alone will cause them to pull back some. They'll start thinking about what other people, most specifically their wives, will think. Is that you too? If you actually told your wife how you are feeling next time she asks, are you worried about what she might think?

If so, you're in good company, because that is exactly what most men think about.

In this world, women are craving for men to wake up and risk being real. Women want men who are able to exist with their masculine emotions. Your wife wants this as well.

No, she does not want you to become an open–book and an emotional mess. Like so many other new things you might learn, going to any extreme doesn't work. While she does want you to embrace your masculine emotions, she doesn't want you to lose your strong logical traits.

Now you need to prepare for people, including your wife, to be shocked when you do this. The truth has a tendency to do that, to shock people. So yes there will be some strange looks, there will be some strange replies, there will be some silence, but that's ok.

Embrace your power in that moment; understand that your truth has rocked their world. When you get used to it, and when they get used to it, suddenly you find yourself holding an entirely new form of power.

Wield that power with care.

The goal of these chapters, the reason for this book is to give you new perspectives and new ideas you can put into action in your own life. Since I talk about the Big Issues, much of what you learn in these chapters will take time to implement, which you can choose to start today.

The choice is always yours.

Fourteen

A ROOM FULL OF WOMEN

*T*he title of this chapter is unfortunately the truth at most churches, at least here in the United States. If you look at the seats and the pews, you see lots of women, and not that many men. Often the men who are there look like they were dragged in, forced to be there for one reason or another.

That is not what the church is supposed to be.

This unfortunate truth makes perfect sense, if you think about it beyond the surface level.

When most men think about the church, what comes to mind are thoughts about rules, about judgment, about structure, about limitations, and about being told what they can and cannot do.

That is definitely not appealing to men. Men are not looking for yet another set of rules or limitations controlling them. Men are not looking to sit in a room and feel judged; the world already seems to do that well enough.

So of course, most men are not really going to connect in the average church. That makes total sense. Who really wants to go a place where all you hear is what you're not supposed to do and to be judged? I'm a guy of deep faith and even I would be uncomfortable in that setting and would want to bolt for the door.

Instead, I want you to consider this…

Consider that this current reality of most churches is not what the church was intended to be. Jesus did not come to give humankind a completely new set of rules and restrictions. Jesus did not come to look a man in the eye and condemn him.

In another chapter, I'll comment on the image of Jesus that so many have grown up with. The Jesus of the Bible is not simply the mild–mannered and soft man you might think he is. He is the man you want by your side through any battle…

To make matters worse, the modern church seems to want to make men more feminine, in that these are the lessons and messages that are so often taught during the church services: be meek, be kind, be giving, be gentle, be passive, be willing to lose for the greater good. Now all of those can be real positive messages, which is important, but what is missing is the other side, the side for men.

When was the last time you visited a church and you heard messages about power, about victory, about defeating your enemies, about sex, about anger, about carrying your sword, about winning a battle, about spiritual warfare, about leadership, about courage, about strength, and on and on…? All of those messages are just as much part of the teaching in the Bible, but they seem to be absent in the church's message to men.

To pile on this more, men also avoid a place where truth isn't really taught. Men can sniff out the fakeness of a sermon quickly. Even if they are not bible scholars and don't exactly know why it seems fake, they can tell. If the leader of the church is "too good", if the leader never shares any honest challenges or struggles, then what is there for the man to identify with?

I know that too many pastors will talk about their own struggles and weaknesses the same way so many answer the job interview question, "tell me about your weakness". Do men really want to learn from a pastor who says his main weakness is that he works too hard, or that he cares too much?

Nope, pastors have the same struggles as the rest of us men. Pastors have challenges with porn, with debt, with lust, with anger, with aggression, with confusion, with pride, with ego, and have questions about their own faith. When was the last time you heard any pastor admit these, or even touch on these subjects? It seems like the only time they are touched on is when the pastor tells everyone that these are sins, that they are wrong, and that you should avoid such things.

Wow, thanks for the insight. That was helpful... and why should I be here again? I don't need to be here surrounded by judgement and someone too good to talk to me about my real struggles.

Think about the fakeness you see in many church leaders, and then think about what Jesus said here:

"While Jesus was having dinner at Matthew's house, many tax collectors and sinners came and ate with him and his disciples. When the Pharisees saw this, they asked his disciples, "Why does your teacher eat with tax collectors and sinners?"

On hearing this, Jesus said, "It is not the healthy who need a doctor, but the sick. But go and learn what this means: "I desire mercy, not sacrifice." For I have not come to call the righteous, but sinners."

(A different version states the last line as, "I have not come to call respectable people, but outcasts." I like that line better.)

If you feel closer to the outcast, then you are in good company, and you are exactly the kind of man that Jesus was talking about. You're the kind of guy I am and talk to: we are the outcasts!

Now I know this message might seem too negative for some, but that isn't my intention. My intention is to shine a light on a problem, on a challenge for the church.

More than that, for you specifically, it is to shine a light on why church may have never connected with you in the past. You may have only been exposed to the feminine side of the church and only have ever known the incomplete portrayal of Jesus, and you knew, in your gut, that the pastor was a bit too good and didn't relate to you and your life.

I ask that you open your mind to the possibility that maybe—just maybe—there is more, that the church is more, and that you can grow and experience more in this life through your faith.

The power of connecting with God is amazing. The power of the connection to Jesus, that you can have simply by asking, is incredible.

Be open and willing to ask, and you may be amazed at where you go.

Fifteen

IS THIS YOUR HELL ON EARTH?

How do you define your own hell on Earth?

Imagine this situation:

You wake up in the morning, just like any other day. You drag yourself out of bed, take a shower, get dressed, eat breakfast, and head into your job. There you sit at your desk and repeat the exact same things that you did yesterday, knowing that's what you're going to repeat tomorrow. You listen to the exact same conversations from your co-workers that you know you're going to hear tomorrow. So far all the same as you were expecting, just another day in a long line of days.

You get your morning coffee, to break free from your cube for a while, pass by the same people as you did yesterday, nod hello to the same people as you will tomorrow, head back to your desk for the rest of the morning, and then finally it is time to escape for your lunch break.

That's where it happens. At lunch, you bump into someone very familiar.

Because that someone is you, only he is a different version of you. He looks like you, he sounds like you, he walks like you (although there is more confidence in how he walks and how he talks), he seems to be just like you, but something is clearly different, he isn't you.

You meet the version of you who has made the changes that you know you should be making; this version of you has been living his life to the fullest. He has failed in spectacular ways and then risen again, he has painfully lost and then won again, he has created powerful goals and reached them, he is fully living as a significant man.

Imagine you standing there, in stunned silence, as this other you is right there in front of you, clearly living life on his terms. He waves to his wife and kids, out there in the awesome car you have always dreamed of driving.

He tells you of all the great work he has done. He tells you of the lives he has impacted. He tells you of what he has created and what he has built. He tells you how he leads his (your) family. He tells you about the passionate relationship he has with his (your) wife. He tells you about his powerful connection with God. He tells you about the amazing home he lives in. He tells you about all the people that he has been able to help with his business. He tells you about all of it, and how he got there.

A tear comes to your eye, as you realize just how close you really were… you were just some key choices away, some key investments away, some key conversations away, and some key actions away.

But, you decided to play it safe and small. You chose not to have those conversations, you chose not to make those investments, and you chose not to take any of those actions. You chose to let your excuses keep their power over you. You chose not to take any risk, and you chose not to try anything new.

You chose to keep things as they were, thinking that was as good as life could be for you, even while you were haunted by the "is this all there is?" question.

If only you knew how close you really were. If only you did something about it.

There you stand, staring directly into the face of what was quite literally yours for the taking; looking at all that you could have had and what you could have accomplished.

The other version of you looks at you with sadness in his eyes, as he too knew what could have been. After all, he is living it right now. He was at the exact same place you were at, he had to make the same tough choices, he had to have the same conversations, he had to decide to invest in himself, he had to take action, and he did.

He shakes your hand, and then he walks out to your dream car, he gets in and he drives off with your smiling wife and your happy kids.

Seeing what could have been your reality, knowing how close it was but that you chose not to really go after what you wanted, realizing that it was all within your grasp, but you didn't take it…

…that is your hell on Earth.

How could you go back to your life, as it was, after that encounter? Imagine the frustration you would be feeling, every single day, knowing what was there for you; knowing what could have been yours? Imagine returning to your cube while being aware that the other you was out there enjoying his afternoon doing what he wanted, fully in control of his own future?

And today, here you are, in that exact place and time where you get to decide, where you get to choose, where you get to pick the man you will become.

Only now it isn't a story, now it isn't fiction. It is real, very real. The man in this story is you, and right now, you are standing at the crossroads. You are, right now, the man who gets to make new choices about his life.

Which man, which version of you, will you choose to be? As I asked in an earlier chapter, who do you have to become? Are you going to be the current you, the man who is content to remain as he is, or are you going to be the other you, who you met at lunch, the man who is living a significant life?

Either way you get to choose, and you get to live with the results of that choice.

Choose wisely.

Sixteen
THE EASY TRAP AND YOUR WIFE

At first, it doesn't seem like a trap at all.

If you've been working on something for a while, maybe a hobby like woodworking, shooting at the range, playing an instrument, taking care of your car, or anything really… there is a trap.

When you have something that you have done for a while, something that now seems to come easy to you, something that you can practically do in your sleep, that is when you need to watch out.

Easy can very quickly become a trap, even though at first it doesn't seem like a trap at all.

After all, we all like easy, right? We want things to come to us easily, we want to figure things out easily, we want to solve our challenges easily, and so on… All of that is true, yes we like and enjoy when things come easy to us.

Easy isn't something to avoid, it isn't something to think about as a negative. I'm not suggesting that easy is bad. If we never had anything easy in life, our lives would become quite the burden, with constant struggle and challenge every single day. So no, easy isn't something you should equate with bad.

However, easy can absolutely become a trap, if you open your mind to see the trap.

The reason for this is that when we have crossed the line and something comes easy to us, we all have a tendency to slow down, to relax, and to stop reaching for the next level. When things become easy we feel like we have made it, and we have reached that place we wanted to go or we have learned all that we wanted to learn.

That's why, at first, it doesn't seem like a trap.

When you reach that place, you, me, we, all of us, can have this time, this feeling, where we sigh a big sigh of relief (or scream out in joy) that we made it.

And you know what? You should feel that and you should do that! You should scream out in joy, you should sigh in relief, and you should take in everything and fully embrace your accomplishment. You should sit back and appreciate what you have done, what you have learned, and how you have changed. You should appreciate all you had to do to get where you are. You should do all of that and you should soak it all in.

After that however, that is where you will find the trap lurking in the shadows. That is where you can become stuck. All too often, once we get to that place, or we have reached that goal, that is where we stay. When we hit that point, we can easily stop reaching for more, stop learning more, and stop looking to new heights.

You can quickly get stuck in the trap of easy, which can quickly lead to you being lazy and simply not trying to grow, learn, or do anything else that will push you to your next level.

Without paying attention to it, you can have a month, year, or decade go by where you have not moved forward at all, because you were stuck in the easy trap. It was so comfortable, it required so little of your effort anymore that you could do it automatically, and you forgot that you wanted to go even higher. You forgot that there was another part of the mountain to climb.

Imagine that you wanted to run a marathon, and during your training, you became excellent at running the half-marathon. People came to see you run, they even gave you awards, and running a half-marathon became so easy for you that you stopped training and preparing for the full marathon. You forgot that was something that you had ever wanted, so many years ago. Instead, you just ran the easy race, the half–marathon that you can now run without even doing any real training at all.

Take some time, right now, and think about the areas of your life where things are easy for you. It could be in a relationship, could be an area of your work, could be a hobby, or anything. What is some part of your life where things come to you easily, without much effort on your part at all?

With that in your mind now, think about what it would take to get to the next level of that thing, whatever it happens to be. What will you have to learn? Who will you have to talk with? Who will you have to become? What are you going to have to do to get there?

Can you see how quickly easy can become a trap? If you're like me, and most other men I've spoken with about this, the idea of staying where things are easy sure seems, well easier. That's the point

This is especially true with men and their relationships with their wives. If things are ok and easy now, they would rather not risk doing what is needed to get to that next level. They would rather not have the hard conversations and make the required changes to get there. They would rather fall back into the easy and familiar place of today. However, a significant man doesn't live like that. A significant man is not satisfied to have an easy relationship, he wants more, he wants that powerful and intimate connection to his wife and he is willing to do the work to get there. He knows about the trap and he doesn't want to live there, he is always seeking a greater level and he is always trying to get better.

What part of your relationship with your wife is easy now, and could become powerfully epic? Are you taking the easy way out in the bedroom, or are you willing to move out of that trap and have the intimate connection with your wife become amazing?

What about you? Does this very idea, of having new conversations with your wife seem overwhelming? If so, again that's the whole point. That means you are in the easy trap right now. It is time for you to choose to escape the grip of the trap, and refuse to get stuck there.

You can't let yourself fall into the trap of easy. You need to keep on going. Yes, enjoy what you have done, be proud, but don't become complacent. Don't be willing to sit back and let that place of easy become a trap for you to stop moving forward.

Keep learning, keep taking risks, and keep going.

Seventeen

THE INCREDIBLE POWER OF YOUR WHY

When I'm talking with a man about some goal he has (it could be financial, relationships, health, or any goal in any area of his life), most of the time when we finally start getting down into the heart of the discussion, he has the core point backwards.

In fact, most people have this point backwards.

If I'm in a room of 100 men and I ask them something, for example about how to make more money in their business, and ask, "Who wants to know how to do that?" most of the time nearly every hand goes up.

While that seems like the right question to want to have answered… it isn't.

Virtually nothing happens because of *how* to do something, anything, everything… Knowing how to do that thing has very little impact on your ability to actually do it. Knowing how to reach a goal has a tiny influence on you actually reaching that goal. Knowing how to do something has almost no influence on you deciding to do the work of implementing the how that you have learned.

Do overweight people know how to lose weight? Of course. I was someone who was very overweight and I knew how. Eat less and exercise more. There, the end. That is how. Now that you know the how, what has changed? Anything? Is that enough? Is the scale any different? Of course not.

Want to earn more money? Great, here is how. Either do your job well enough to receive a raise at work, or open a business selling some goods or services, with enough of a margin to earn the profit that you desire. Want more how? All right, we can get into the specifics of how to setup an S–Corp or an LLC, how to create a website, how to develop a product line, how to perform market research, how to properly identify a target market, and on and on... Does knowing how to do any of that actually mean you have now made more money? Nope, you've not earned one additional penny, your bank account has yet to see any change, even though you have learned all this how.

You see the power, the real power; it is actually in your *why* it is not in your *how*.

If you don't have a powerful enough *why*, nothing really changes. If you don't have a powerful enough why, even if you make a temporary change, you will reverse back to where you started, and again nothing really changes (other than an increase in your frustration level, because you have all this how and nothing changed). If you don't have a why that is driving you, a why that is keeping you awake at night, and a why that energizes you when you wake up in the morning, yet again nothing will really change.

Give me a man who has a powerful why, and I know that he will succeed, no matter the amount of how that he has in his life. I know that he will follow through on what I offer him and what I teach him. I know that he will do whatever he needs to do in order to reach his goal, smash through, and get to the next level. I know that he will make new choices and make new changes to get there. I know that he will take action on what he learns.

On the other hand, give me a man who doesn't have a powerful why, and I know that no amount of training, information, or detailed how will change anything in his life. Without the why driving him, the how will have little, to no, influence on where he goes or who he becomes.

Imagine that I tell you how to drive from New York to Los Angeles, including some key places to stop along the way. I tell you how to get there in plenty of detail, every road, every turn, every gas station, and every place to eat and to sleep. I give you how details of every single part of the trip. You are filled to the top with the how to drive from NY to LA. Does that make you want to take that drive? No? Why not?

On the other hand, imagine that I merely suggest you might want to drive from New York to Los Angeles, and that along the way in each of those key places to stop you can find a two–digit number. Then I tell you that when you get to LA you will use those two–digit numbers to open a safe that has five million dollars cash inside. Finally, I tell you that the first person to make the drive and get the safe combination will receive the money.

Do you want to take that drive now, even though I didn't really tell you any of the how details? I thought your answer might have changed.

What is different between those two scenarios? By now, you should be able to see that clearly, the difference is that one is about the how and the other is about the why. When the why matters, the how actually becomes nearly irrelevant in you reaching your objective. If the why is powerful enough, you will do whatever you need to on the how side.

If you want to earn more money, really think about why you want to. If you want to lose weight, really think about why you must lose weight. If you want to connect with God, why is that? If you want a more intimate relationship with your wife, why do you have to have that?

Each why must be powerful and clear. It is not enough to say, "Because I want to". It is not enough to say, "Because I think it would be nice". Those are weak answers, which will not drive you forward with any long–term change.

Until you have a seriously powerful why behind those wants, your wants are just empty dreams and nothing more. Sorry to say that so harshly, but it is the truth. Simply wanting something isn't going to lead you to doing what you need to do to get that something in your life.

Take some real time to think about these questions:

Why do you want to lead a significant life? Why do you want to be that sort of man? Why are you going to be willing to do whatever you have to do, in order to become that man? Why are you going to invest in yourself? Why does it matter to your wife? Why does it matter to your kids? Why does it matter to your grandchildren?

Why?

When you are able to create a powerful enough why, you then can use that as a driving force, use it as a means to keep you going when the motivation wears off, which it will. When you don't feel like doing the work on those hard days, you go back to your why, clearly remember your why, and let that pull you up the next step.

Your why truly has incredible power. Use it!

Eighteen
HIS ONE DECISION THAT CHANGED EVERYTHING

I want to tell you the story of a man named Joe. His name is Joe, but it could just as easily be any other man you'll see today, or maybe even you. Imagine this…

Joe tried hard to be a good man. He had been married for a while, and he has two young children, one daughter and one son. He had been working hard for years to make ends meet for his family.

However, something was wrong. His life was not going the way he thought it would. He was not making enough money. He had zero relationship with God. He was not connecting with his wife; she was more like a roommate. His kids didn't even really know who he was; they were more like strangers.

In fact, he didn't even know who he was anymore. He was a hollow shell of the man he expected that he would become. He was nowhere near who he thought he would be by now.

Joe was moving through the motions of life, but he was not alive. He had lost all sense of adventure and happiness. He had lost his joy and had lost his enthusiasm for, well, everything.

He was no longer fighting. He wasn't fighting for his relationship, he wasn't fighting for his career, he wasn't even fighting for himself anymore.

Soon he found himself sitting at a large table, meeting in a lawyer's office, looking down at the pile of paperwork about his upcoming divorce.

Life got very ugly, seemingly very fast. The arguments came one after the other, about the kids, the house, the cars, and the bank accounts; every conversation seemed to become an argument. Even talking about the pets quickly turned into an argument.

During this time Joe had become so distracted by the overwhelming weight of it all that his performance at his job, the one that gave him no joy anyway, suffered and he was laid off during a round of cut backs.

So there sat Joe. He had lost his job, his income, his marriage, his children, his home, and he had lost his identity.

It was that last one that hurt the most, he had lost his own sense of purpose, of meaning, and of identity. He felt like a fraud, as if he was walking around in a costume that looked like a man on the outside, but he knew he was nothing on the inside.

In searching through how to solve this problem, in thinking about how he could make things better for everyone, he finally did make a decision. A decision that changed everything.

This decision he was certain would allow everyone involved be at peace. This decision he was sure would let everyone move forward, not having to be burdened by his misery any longer.

He took the time and he planned what would happen, he carefully thought through his decision, and on a rainy Tuesday morning, he followed through and he ended his own life with a shotgun.

He thought he was making things easier for everyone, he thought he was making the situation better, that his death would improve the world and the lives of all involved.

Joe ended up leaving his son and daughter to spend their entire lives wondering, "Why?" or even worse, asking themselves if they were somehow to blame for their father's decision.

Joe ended up leaving his ex-wife with an incredible burden to carry.

Joe ended up leaving only pain, confusion, sadness, anger, and sorrow when he thought he was leaving everyone and everything better.

But here is the thing guys, it didn't have to happen like this for Joe. He didn't have to take that way out. He didn't have to make that decision.

A permanent solution to a temporary problem is never the way out, ever.

We have a serious problem in our world when men feel so lost, so hurt, so miserable, so broken, so undeserving, and so trapped that they think that the best solution is for them to remove themselves from the equation itself.

The world needs men. Families need men. Women need men. Children need men. Men need men.

The world needs you. Families need you. Women need you. Children need you. Men need you.

That is the truth, even if it doesn't seem like it today. Even if it feels like only darkness today, that is still the truth. The world needs you, you have more to do, more to offer, more to experience.

Men have to be willing to step into that truth and be willing to learn from the past as they move into the future.

If you have messed up, ok. Own that and use it to build on. If you have hurt others, ok. Own that and use that as you grow into a better man. If you have hurt yourself, ok. Own that and allow it to become a primary building block as you learn and grow.

It is time for you to forgive those who have hurt you. It is time for you to forgive those who didn't understand you.

Most importantly, it is time to forgive yourself.

But do not take that permanent solution to the temporary problem. As dark as it may seem, the darkness never lasts forever, the light always comes back. There is always a way out of the pit, there is always an opportunity to look up to the blue sky after the storm has passed.

Always.

Choose to forgive yourself, and choose the light.

PS—If you're in that dark place right now, if you're thinking about this decision, I'm asking you to please call 800–273–TALK (8255). There is someone waiting to talk to you right now, 24 hours a day seven days a week. You might think no one cares, but I do. Please call. You are worth it. Your life does matter.

Nineteen

TIME FOR YOU TO BELIEVE AGAIN

I t happens to all of us, at some point.

Every man will hit the wall, at some time during his life. That place where it seems that nothing is working, that you're making no progress, that you are just spinning in place never moving forward, and that life will be like that forever.

Even worse, some of us will end up falling into the pit. That place of darkness where it seems that all has been lost. This is a dangerous place, and one that I wish no man would ever experience, but I know that many do.

It happened to me. I lost my house, my business, my income, my life savings, and worst of all I had lost my own identity as a man. Every day, the act of climbing out of bed was a struggle, a challenge that seemed like climbing Mount Everest instead of the simple task it was for the rest of the world. Every day the basic and mundane tasks were gigantic challenges.

I understand hitting the wall and falling into the pit, I understand being in those places. And I also understand that being in those places is not permanent, it is not where you have to spend the rest of your life. Notice that line carefully, those aren't places where you "have to" spend the rest of your life.

Today you stand in a place where you can create a new future for yourself, just as I have shared earlier in this book. Today you stand at the crossroads where you get to make new powerful choices.

Maybe you've been beaten down, maybe you've been hurt, maybe you've been crushed, maybe you've been lost, and maybe you think you have been so far down into that pit that you have no options and you think that today is how the rest of your life is going to be.

Well, it isn't. It. Isn't.

It is time to stop being that guy who is living his life broken. It's time to stop being the guy who only sees the things that people and the world have done to you. It's time to stop telling yourself that life would be better once everyone else starts doing what you think they are supposed to be doing.

It is time for you to open your mind to new thoughts. New ideas. New realities.

The simple truth is that you can become the significant man you know you have inside. The simple truth is that you can reclaim the power you have lost in order to become that man.

Simple truths, yes. However, you need to do the work, you need to step up, you need to wake up, and you need to accept that you really can reclaim this power.

It starts with you. It all begins with you deciding that you have had enough, that you are no longer willing to lie there and let life roll over you. It begins with you deciding that as of today your answer to the inner voice talking down to you is, "No More!"

Today is the day you can decide that you will not take it anymore, and that you will not go quietly into the night. Today is the day you decide to rise up and stand for yourself.

It is time for you to believe again. To believe that you can do this, that you do not need to live in the pit the rest of your life.

You were not created to struggle. You were not created to live down in that pit of darkness. That is not what God had in mind for you when He created you.

You were created to be a Hero. You were created to be a Warrior. You were created to be a Leader.

You were created for amazing things. You were created for greatness. You were created for significance. You already have all that inside, even if it has been buried so far down you don't see it right now.

It begins, as you're learning that so many other critical changes do, with a choice. You need to choose to believe again. You need to choose to believe that you do have greatness and power inside you. You need to choose to believe that you do have the ability to become the significant man that you were created to be.

Will this take work? Of course it will, you've lived long enough to know that. You're smart enough to know there is no magical overnight miracle solution. You're wise enough to know that you will have to do the work to get where you want to go.

Will you stumble and fall, while you are growing and climbing out of the darkness? Of course, you've got enough experience to know that too. You're smart enough and wise enough to know this reality as well.

But will that stop you? No, it won't, because this time you believe in you. You are focusing on where you are going, not where you have been or even where you are today.

Your past will not stop you. You will look back on those times of pain and confusion and realize what they really were all along: they were disguised lessons teaching you some of the most important lessons of your entire life. You will look back at that pit and realize how much you learned on the way down and how much you learned on the way up.

It is time for you to believe again.

Twenty

MAYBE YOU NEED MORE PAIN

*I*t's an odd thing to say that you might need more pain, I understand that. A long time ago, the first time I ever said those words to one of the guys I was mentoring, they even sounded a bit strange to me.

We were talking about his situation, what he liked in his life, what he didn't like, what he needed to change, how to improve his relationships, how to lead his children, and so on… a great and powerful conversation, like so many I've had with other men over the years.

He was telling me about something in his life that he wished was different, something that he said he wanted to change, but he hadn't been able to yet.

My reply to him was, "Maybe you need more pain."

That left him shocked for a moment, he said nothing and just thought for a while. I'm fine with the silence in conversations, sometimes our best moments come to us during those times when no one is saying a word, and we can just think, so I never push someone during those times.

You see we all have two primary drivers of change in our lives. One is to increase the amount of pleasure we experience, and the other is to decrease the amount of pain we experience.

Note: these two drivers are during our normal and everyday lives, I'm not talking about a man who is in fight-or-flight or true survival mode.

The pain driver is more powerful than the pleasure driver is, by far. As in, this isn't even close. It seems somewhat odd that pain is a more powerful driver than pleasure, because on the surface (think about movies, commercials, TV shows, and other advertising) it looks like we are chasing pleasure. It is a much easier sell to push the pleasure than the pain; it is easier to say, "Buy this product and you'll get these awesome things."

However, when it comes down to changing things in our lives that is when the driver of pain dwarfs the driver of pleasure in our taking action.

Think about your own experiences for a moment. When are you more likely to make a change in your life or in anything significant really? Is it when you have something painful that you need to change now or is it when you are seeking something more pleasure filled that you would like to have in the future?

If you have broken your leg, are you thinking more about getting that pain fixed now, or are you thinking more about how fun it would be to go to rock climbing with your wife later?

If you have broken your leg, are you more likely to go and get that pain treated today, or are you more likely to meet up with your friends to have fun and go off–roading for the weekend?

Which one of those takes priority in your life? Will you have greater urgency in reducing the pain you are experiencing or in adding to the pleasure you desire?

These are extreme examples, on purpose, but you need to realize the same point holds true for your life as it does for your broken leg.

If you are not in enough pain, the odds of you changing anything are quite low. Yes, you can go through a transformation and see life differently. Yes, you can learn to keep leveling up, even when you're not in pain, but that takes time and is actually a different conversation from this one here. So if the idea is to change, but there isn't any real driver behind the idea, the change simply doesn't happen. You can think about this in conjunction with the chapter about the Power Of Your Why.

What this means for you is that if you are in a place right now where you have some certainty and where your day–to–day reality is fixed, but there is nothing truly painful (annoying or "not fun" don't count as painful), then you very likely have some internal barriers to your own changes.

In other words, if you're comfortable with where you are right now, even if the comfort is with something that you don't really like, you will have to work to remove the barriers you have created for yourself. Those barriers are blocking your path to changing the reality of your life.

We can be comfortable with things we don't like. We can get used to situations that are not positive, and we can become resigned to accept them as reality in our lives. When that happens, we become dulled to the pain; the pain is not a driver. The comfort and acceptance of the situation become the internal barriers we have to break through if we want change.

Now I want to be very clear, this does not mean you should go put yourself in a painful situation, and it doesn't mean you should do something stupid that will hurt you, or your family, in order to motivate yourself with pain.

Instead, become aware of this truth: you can "create more pain" in your mind.

To start with, visualize and realize what your next few years and decades will look like if you don't change. Be very exact and specific in your answers. Has your wife given up on you becoming the man she knew you could have been? Have your kids stopped respecting you? What is your son or daughter learning from how you live today? Does your wife no longer look at you with that sparkle and passion in her eyes? How do you feel about zero change in your income level? What about getting even more out of shape?

Think about the Your Hell On Earth chapter. Make those thoughts very real. Once you have visualized and have seen what your life can be, it becomes quite painful not being there. It is painful to know that you can become that man, but you haven't yet. That is one way you can create more pain in your mind.

Use those thoughts as your motivators. Knowing what is just beyond your current reality is a painful reminder for many men. What future are you letting slip through your fingers as you accept things today? How much longer are you willing to waste your potential?

The clearer and the stronger you make those visualizations, the more powerful the reasons you create for your change are, the more likely you are to create powerful changes in your life.

You'll know when you get there, you'll know when those visualizations and reasons are strong enough, because you will be driven to change. You will have had enough of sleepwalking through life. You will have had enough of watching other guys do what you think about. You will have had enough of knowing that your new life is right there, if you are willing to take it.

You'll be irritated that you're not there yet. You'll be annoyed that you have not reached that place yet. You'll be in pain because you know that life is right there and you don't yet have it. You'll wake up in the morning, upset that you have to spend one more day the way you are now.

Then, you will change. And, I'm looking forward to hearing about it.

Twenty-One
WRITE A NEW STORY

Your story hurts you or your story helps you, it is never neutral, and you get to choose which of those is true in your life.

One thing that is common with the men who are part of Significant Man is that they become aware that they've been telling themselves all kinds of stories, and have been doing so for their entire lives. You have been telling yourself your own story from early on in your life, starting as a small child and continuing all the way up through today while you are reading this.

Your stories are quite likely making your life much harder than it needs to be. Your stories can make you miserable, unhappy, unfulfilled, and make you lean towards decisions that not only hurt you, but hurt those around you, all without you ever realizing what is taking place.

Here are some of the things I've heard over the years, all based on stories men tell themselves: I've lost where my power comes from, I've lost my identity, I've become unable to see the light through the dark, and I have lost sight of the life I was created to live.

Those results, those giant ideas and challenges, all come from your stories. Yes, this includes the stories that you have heard, over your entire life. Most importantly however, this comes from the stories that you have been repeating to yourself, about yourself.

- The more you tell a story that you are broken, the more broken you will be.
- The longer that you tell a story you are never going to earn a great income, the longer that will be true.
- The more you tell a story that you can't understand your wife, the more your relationship will be strained.
- The longer that you tell a story that you don't see any reason to connect with God, the longer that painful hole will exist in your heart.
- The more you tell a story that you will never have the car, the house, or the other things you say you want in life, the more that will be your reality.

All from your stories. All from what you keep repeating to yourself.

You have been writing these stories, the ones that you continue to tell yourself, for your entire life. They start early, when you are young, and at that point, the stories tend to be a mirror of what other people say about you. Then, as you get older, you start to fill your own details into your stories.

The stories become how you define yourself. When people ask you about you, these are the stories that you have ready to share at a moment's notice. When someone asks about your career, you tell the story of your career. When someone asks about your wife, you tell the story about your marriage and your relationship to your wife. When someone asks about your children, you tell the story about them.

You've been repeating these stories for as long as you have been thinking about things, and you're really good at sharing them.

Now here is the secret about your stories, and this is seriously powerful: When you are finally ready and open to doing so, you create a new set of stories, you write new chapters, and you finally become the author of the reality that you are living in. Your stories can empower you, if you want them to.

You can have all that you have wanted in your life, in all the areas of your life.

You begin this process with stopping the old stories first. You stop repeating the stories that do not serve you and you refuse to tell any story that will disempower you or put you in a negative light.

Notice I'm not suggesting you lie here, not that at all. Lying creates negativity and uncertainty in your life, it creates confusion and resentment. Do not lie. Instead, you simply stop talking about the negative aspects of your story, stop giving power to and feeding the stories that pull you down.

You no longer say things like, "I'm always taken advantage of.", "I'm never going to have what he has.", "My wife will never understand me." or "It never works for me." Those are all damaging stories, they are very powerful, and they become definitional stories you repeat about yourself. You need to remove them from your language immediately.

Now you need to realize that you don't just jump directly from "I'm a miserable entrepreneur." all the way to, "I'm the best entrepreneur to walk the planet." Because your subconscious will know that isn't reality and will end up working against you, you'll end up sabotaging yourself without realizing it.

Yes, you can make leaps and bounds, but don't be silly about this and think that you can simply make an entire 180 degree shift in who you are as a man in one minute. After all, it took your whole life to get you where you are today, obviously it won't reverse course in what you learn in one short chapter.

You start by silencing the old, negative, harmful, and disempowering stories. Stop yourself in your tracks when you start repeating them. Do not let yourself continue to talk about yourself like that. From there you move on to building positive and empowering stories.

In other words, the first step is to stop with the old negative stories. Do not give those stories any more power, don't give them any more life, don't give them any opportunity to keep growing in your mind. Stop speaking life into those negative stories.

Once you become quicker at catching your old negative stories, and stopping them, then you start working on the new stories. You create new ones that build you up and that fill you with positive energy and the powerful feelings you deserve.

Begin with stories like, "I'm a positive person.", "I find opportunity in every situation." or "I keep learning and growing every day." Create and build these positive stories, ones that are unique and specific to you and your life. Return the power to you, on purpose. Take the power back and use it to create these new stories.

Yes, this takes time and practice to put into place, but in your gut, you know it is true and something that you have to start doing. It is time to write yourself a new story.

Twenty-Two

ARE YOU REALLY WILLING TO TELL THE TRUTH?

O ne thing that is a powerful reality for the man who is on his journey towards becoming a significant man is to stop lying and tell the truth. It might sound easy, but it isn't.

As men, we have built up walls and barriers all over our worlds. Walls around our emotions. Barriers around our ideas. Walls around our feelings. Barriers around our thoughts.

And serious walls around our hearts.

Most of us men would much rather keep our hearts guarded than ever risk letting them be broken. This is something most women, including our wives, don't really realize. The pain and heartache can be so great that we would far prefer building incredible barriers around our hearts than ever open them to the possibility of them being broken. Therefore, men lie to themselves and others about what they really want and need in their hearts and in their lives.

Most men would rather keep building up the story and the lie about how great their life is, how they already have it all, how they are already on the right path, and on and on… So men lie about their current life, not willing to let anyone inside the shell, not willing to let anyone see behind the mask, because it is safer to live that way.

We can't really live like that forever, none of us; I can't live like that and you can't live like that, eventually the barriers shatter. We can't exist and fully live a significant life with all those walls, all those barriers, and our true selves kept locked up inside. Because that means we are not living the truth. We are not living in the real power we have, as men.

The hardest part, as you learn to work through this, is when you end up confronted with the lies that you have been telling yourself about yourself. If you've built up a false story about who you are, what you do, how you live, and you have also shared that with the world, you'll have to live that life to maintain the story. You'll believe it on the surface, all the while knowing the truth behind the lie.

Then you hit the point where you are literally living a lie. Too often, this sort of lie is so deep and the man is so much "part of the lie" that only he knows, down deep in his gut, that his life is a lie. He might be financing his entire life on credit cards and with a second (or third) mortgage. He might be spending every day at a job he hates. He might be pretending to have it all together, while he is teetering on the edge of chaos and depression. His wife probably has no idea just how far down into the lie their life really is until the day everything crashes and it all goes horribly wrong.

You see a life built on lies simply cannot last, it will always go wrong and it will always come crashing down. When that life has affected others, most often meaning a wife and kids (but also other family members, friends, co–workers, and business associates), they will all end up going down with the ship as well; their lives thrown into the chaos.

Since us men tend to not open up and talk about these things, it becomes even harder to work through the lies and start living in the power of truth. When you feel like there is no one in your life who can walk by your side and have your back, then taking the first step seems nearly impossible.

However, you have to do it. If you have any desire, at all, to start embracing the powerful life you have inside, you must build your life on a foundation of truth. There is no other way.

It is time to stop building new walls and new barriers around the truth; it is time to stop hiding what your soul is really telling you. It is time let people in to see the real you, and that includes both the positive and negative that you have been hiding. It is time you owned the reality of your life today, and that you owned the reality of the life that you want to be living. That means sharing your reality with those who are close to you, who support you, and who walk with you.

You have to stop lying to yourself about what you really want out of life and about the challenges that you are facing. You have to stop lying about what you want, what you are addicted to, what hurts you, what scares you, what drives you, about your hopes, your dreams, and the life you have hidden inside.

While this is an old saying that sometimes sounds a bit cliché, it is extremely relevant and holds incredible power to you: "The Truth Shall Set You Free"

You have to live a life of truth. This means truth with your business, truth with your co-workers, truth with your kids, truth with your friends, and absolutely yes—truth with your wife.

Beyond that, you have to live a life of truth with yourself. You have to live a life of integrity, a life where you are living the truth every single day.

When you do this, you are taking a giant weight off your back; you are lifting the burden from your shoulders. It will not be easy. It will not be painless. After all, you have been building your life on these lies from when you were young, and strong walls and barriers don't come down easily.

Do know that this isn't optional. In my events when we get to this sort of conversation, I expect resistance, and I expect honesty. When someone suggests they have nothing like this to deal with, they have no lies in their life, I know they aren't ready. And that's ok, we are all walking our own walk and dealing with our own stuff in our own times. But this isn't an option. If you want to live the life of a significant man, the lies have to end.

Be willing to take the risk to live a life of truth.

Twenty-Three
SOME OF MY DEEP TRUTH

To begin with, I have an upfront edit to this chapter. I received the following feedback, based on what you are about to read:

"Warren, you talk about truth, but you are sharing a message that is just "some" of your deep truth. What are you hiding from us? This doesn't really seem like telling the full truth. Why not just share it all? Or are you one of those guys who doesn't lead by example?"

To the person who wrote this, I appreciate your feedback. It shows you are reading and paying attention, so I thank you for that.

I am sharing only some of my deep truth for a few reasons. First is time. No one is going to read an entire chapter that is nothing other than a list of what I've done wrong in the past and the mistakes I've made. Not to mention that would end up a depressing hundred pages by the time I was done! Beyond the issue of time however, some conversations are best to have in person. Conversations where we can look each other in the eye, and hear one another's voices. I hide nothing; the guys I work with know that everything is on the table. If you and I ever are able to share that type of conversation, I will honor and value what you have to share.

OK, that being said, let's get started…

In the last chapter, I talked about lies and truth, and talked about how important it is for you to be willing to tell the truth. This "telling the truth thing" is hard for most people, and can sometimes seem like an impossible idea for men.

As a side note. Ladies if you are reading along here, you need to have some context here. This same point applies to you; you have to confront your lies just as your husband does. Men are *not* out there purposefully lying to you or anyone else; please read the prior chapter for reference. Most men really are trying hard to live the life of a good man and do the right thing for you and your family. I'm not talking about some pathological liar who is only trying to get ahead himself and not caring about hurting other people. I want this point to be clear.

All right, so let me go first.

For the longest time I was the stereotypical successful entrepreneur. I had a real company (with partners, investors, offices on three continents, employees, the whole deal) and, from the outside, everything looked great. I had an amazing house, which my family and I literally built with our own hands. I was flying across oceans to deliver talks. I had a wonderful wife and incredible kids.

Inside however, I was not happy. I was playing the part, but I was not honest with myself or anyone else. I had built this life around me, trapping myself inside the story. I could feel things slipping away. I could feel things were about to spiral out of control. But, being the stubborn man I was, I would not give in. I would not give up the story and tell the truth.

Eventually, of course, it all crashed and burned (it always does guys, always). Within a very short time, I lost the house, the business, and every penny of the family savings. We went from limo rides and five-star restaurants to my family sharing a meal at Taco Bell, paid for with loose change, for a special treat.

The worst part was that I became lost as a man. I had lost my own identity. I felt as if my entire life was a failure. I had failed at my business, my home, my income, and now I had even failed as a husband and a father; I was not providing for my wife and children.

That was the hardest part, losing my identity as a man. My wife tried her best to help, she is an incredible and amazing woman, but I was in such a bad place I couldn't even really hear and see what she had to offer. And the spiral down continued. It was a dark time for me. I'll share plenty more about what I went through personally then, if we have an opportunity to talk to one another someday. In a short summary, there is a reason I understand and can talk to men about depression, suicide, and fighting the enemy of this world. I've seen that darkness face to face.

I was humbled and humiliated. My ego and pride were totally devastated. In order to have food on the table, I had to accept help from our local church and food pantry. I had to seek out the local special assistance plan our city offered to keep the utilities on as they were about to be turned off and I had no way of paying them. The family van was so far behind in payments that it was due for repossession and I had to keep it hidden to make sure it wasn't hauled away.

As I said, it was a very dark place. And yes, this is still just "some" of my truth!

The point here guys is that years ago I would have never shared this. I would have written something about how great things always are and have been. I may have written some post or created a meme about how adversity makes you stronger, all without telling you any of mine. I would have been that guy who doesn't share any problems, pretending that there really aren't any in my life.

Remember back in the chapter about A Room Full of Women, when I mention how men so dislike the pastor who never shares any real burden or struggle... yeah I was that guy for the longest guy. Which is also why I can see through those guys so easily now.

The turning point for me in what I have shared with you was when I accepted this truth and was willing to own my reality. For a while, I wasn't even admitting to myself the position that I was in, I couldn't see the danger I had put myself and my family in. Talk about lying to yourself! I was the master at that, without realizing it was happening.

No longer do I hide this story and pretend it never happened. It's true that my family is no longer in that position, the cars are all paid for, dinner doesn't have to be Taco Bell anymore, and so on... it wouldn't be hard to just skip over this part of my past or pretend it never happened. But this is part of who I am.

More than part of who I am though, it is why I do what I do. I am fully convinced that had I not gone through that painful season of life I would not be able to work with men to the level that I now can. I would not have the same perspective and understanding that I now do. I would not have the same appreciation for what it takes to climb out of the darkness that I now do. I would not be able to see the danger in seeking success in money and business.

It is 100% correct to state that the Significant Man work I do today, including this book, would not exist had I not experienced what I did.

So my friend, this is what it looks like when you share some of your deep truth.

If you want to keep moving on your journey towards living the life of a significant man, you have to tell the truth.

Now you need to get to it, open up and share your truth as well.

Twenty-Four
THE ULTIMATE WARRIOR

We're shifting gears here, moving away from the stuff I've shared over the last few chapters.

Today I am going to talk about The Ultimate Warrior. I'm going to talk about the one man who you want to have on your side. The one man you want to have with you, when you are down in the trenches, fighting for your life. The one man you want to have your back when you are facing your enemies.

This probably is not the man you're thinking of, and this probably is not the man you expect me to pick.

I'm not picking the easy answer and saying it should be your best friend or your father. While those are certainly great men to have on your side, neither of them are The Ultimate Warrior.

I'm not picking the soldier you knew from school, the soldier you know now, the soldier in your family, or even the soldier you yourself might be. Nope, none of them.

I'm not picking the massive football player you knew, or the bar bouncer, or even the MMA fighter that you're friends with. Nope, none of them.

I am picking a man you have heard of before, but you probably don't fully know (I'm still working to fully know him better myself). I am picking a man who has had only part of his story commonly shared with the world.

- This man was feared by governments and leaders.
- This man would make his enemies run away before facing him.
- This man would have his name known on every continent, for thousands of years.

He was a man who hung out with the misfits, the outcasts, and the unworthy men and women of his time. He was a man who chose a handful of rough, uneducated, hard-working fishermen to help tell his message. He was a man who looked the most powerful men of his time in the eye, all while telling them they were wrong. He was a man who did not back down from doing what is right, even when he was mocked and ridiculed.

Who was this man? You might already know, just from this description.

He name is Jesus Christ.

And in my opinion, the modern church has not told His full story, which I think is a big reason why so many men are not interested in church that much these days.

Think about the default image we have of Jesus. We see a man in a flowing robe, beautiful hair, wispy and thin physique, tanned spotless skin, clean sandals, all while sitting on a fluffy cloud with smiling little children all around him.

Ask the average person, even the average church–going person, to describe Jesus and you are likely to hear a list of characteristics like this: nice, kind, gentle, timid, forgiving, peaceful, warm, and meek. Those are all great and important characteristics; I'm not suggesting otherwise at all. I love the fact that those are all part of who He is.

While those are clearly parts of Him and are parts of who He is, they are only parts. People seem to have forgotten the other parts of Him.

Jesus is the Ultimate Warrior.

He could silence entire mobs and crowds with a few words and a look. You think a timid man does that? Of course not.

He could look the most powerful men of the time in the face, and correct them. You think a weakling does that? Of course not.

Do you know that Jesus is called the Lion of Judah? Do you think of a lion as meek? Of course not.

He was a man who knew His mission and would walk with confidence directly into the face of those He challenged. You think a wimp does that? Of course not.

He was a man who upset the authorities and rulers of His time so much that they set out to kill Him. Do you think a quiet nice man does that? Of course not.

He was a man who willingly walked into the trial that He knew would end with his execution. Do you think a coward does that? Of course not.

Let me ask you this. Do you know how the Bible describes the return of Jesus?

Here is how He is described:

"I saw heaven standing open and there before me was a white horse, whose rider is called Faithful and True. With justice he judges and wages war. His eyes are like blazing fire, and on his head are many crowns. He has a name written on him that no one knows but he himself. He is dressed in a robe dipped in blood, and his name is the Word of God. The armies of heaven were following him, riding on white horses and dressed in fine linen, white and clean. Coming out of his mouth is a sharp sword with which to strike down the nations. "He will rule them with an iron scepter." He treads the winepress of the fury of the wrath of God Almighty. On his robe and on his thigh he has this name written: King of Kings and Lord of Lords."

Now that is The Ultimate Warrior! Imagine that man having your back when you go into battle. You're facing your enemy, and then He rides in behind you on His horse, eyes blazing like fire, dressed in a robe that is dipped in blood, with the armies of heaven following him! On top of all that, He is wielding a sword that He can use to strike down entire nations. Yes, that is the most powerful of warriors; no one else comes close.

We rarely get to see and hear about this side of Jesus. We aren't taught enough about how He stands up to injustice, how He got angry at those who turned the church into a robbers' den and drove them out with a weapon that He made for Himself, how He stays true to His purpose through adversity, pain, and challenge, how He battles abuse of authority, how He confronts oppression, how He goes against established religion, or how He made his enemies shake with fear with just His presence.

That is who He is, just as much as He is peaceful, kind, and loving.

If more men realized just who He is, I'm willing to bet that more men would want him on their side. If you don't know Him yet, I suggest you do. There is so much more to Him than you might know.

I am proud of knowing Him, and proud of learning more about Him all the time. And when the challenges come, when I go into battle, I know that standing behind me is The Ultimate Warrior.

I know He has my back, and that is amazing.

Twenty-Five
ARE YOU A REAL MAN?

*A*s men, we've heard the phrase "real man" our whole lives. But, who exactly is a real man?

Is it the stereotypical macho guy, who feels the need to let you know how awesome he is all day long, using women for fun, dominating and acting cold towards children, and driving monster trucks while blowing stuff up to compensate for the hollow feeling he has inside?

Is it the stereotypical sensitive feminine guy, who feels the need to let you know how he feels about everything all day long, making sure that he can cry on demand, also while he is compensating for the feelings he really has inside?

Why does our society seem so eager to tell everyone what a real man really is, even though no one can give you the answer?

That is actually the point here. There isn't a definitive answer as to what a real man is. Even for me, as a man who works with other men all the time, I can tell you there isn't one single answer to this question. I can, however, give you a different perspective on this idea and perhaps give you a different way to think about this question.

I put together a short list of what a real man is for you to think about; these are all characteristics of a real man:

- A real man hurts.
- A real man cries.
- A real man feels.
- A real man loves.
- A real man hates.
- A real man leads.
- A real man learns.
- A real man is tough.
- A real man is strong.
- A real man is complex.
- A real man is powerful.
- A real man is responsible.
- A real man changes the world.
- A real man provides for his family.
- A real man wakes up from his sleep.
- A real man protects those around him.
- A real man stands up for what is right.

You don't have to pretend to be the macho man, and you don't have to go to the opposite end of the spectrum and pretend to be the emotional feminine man. You can simply be who God created you to be. However, what you do have to do is live fully, be open to the full masculine experience, and embrace every part of who you really are.

If you are living a life now where you have to hold everything inside and you are living a life now where you cannot outwardly express your masculinity, then you are going to be conflicted and there will be confusion in your life.

In addition, the other side is also true. If you are living a life that is an emotional open book, where everything is all out there for the world to see and comment on, or if you have moved so far into the feminine, you are also going to be conflicted and there will be confusion in your life.

You have to allow yourself to experience the full range of life itself, without falling too far into one of the extreme ends.

The world needs men to come back into our society. The world needs men who are strong and tough, and who are ready to face adversity. The world needs men who are willing to stop sleepwalking through life. The world needs men who are willing to take chances to become more and do more to benefit themselves, their families, and the world. The world needs men who are willing to open their hearts and admit they want more, to open themselves to the possibility that they can be more, do more, experience more, and become more. And all of that is part of being a real man.

I need to share that someone got upset with me once for saying that a real man hates. That is a complex issue, and one that I admit makes many uncomfortable. The issue is not hate itself; rather the issue is what that hate is focused towards. For me, and those I teach, the goal is to hate evil, never people. Evil is real in this world, and hating evil is not only justified it has biblical basis.

As a significant man, your love for others must be powerful and it must be sincere. While at the same time, you must hate evil. This is an important concept, and one that can take time to comprehend. Too often, we forget that evil and darkness are real enemies of this world, they exist, and their goal is to stop you from becoming a significant man.

So guys, next time you hear the phrase real man, instead of comparing yourself to what someone else says you should be, just think about who you are today and who you are becoming. If you are walking along with everything that I've been sharing in this book, and if you are working to implement what you have been learning, you are becoming a more significant man every day.

And *that* is a real man.

Twenty-Six

YOU CAN'T SAY MASCULINITY IS AWESOME!

Masculinity is awesome! Being a Man is awesome! Yes, I said it, and in our overly politically correct society it seems bizarre that this could be a controversial statement at all.

OK so one thing that I end up dealing with a fair amount is the issue of what masculinity means in our society today. When I bring this up to people, the idea of masculinity itself, there are a few normal replies:

- One is that masculinity is bad, that it is the cause of all the problems in our world.
- Two is that masculinity could be ok, but it really needs to be minimized and controlled in order for there to be any benefit from it.
- Three is that there is actually no such thing as masculinity or femininity, and they are both simple constructs of society and neither really exists.

Well here is my short reply to the idea: Masculinity is very real and is awesome! Yes, awesome!

In the world of today though, you aren't supposed to say things like that. You aren't even supposed to acknowledge that there is an option for masculinity to be awesome, let alone say so.

However, the world needs masculinity. The world needs men, and it needs masculine men.

One of the reasons our society seems to be so mixed up is due to too many people wanting to put down masculinity and too many people telling boys they shouldn't act like boys. That leads to men who are confused about their roles in society and who have no idea how they are supposed to act once they are men.

A society without masculine men is a society that is broken, one that is wandering without direction, without vision, without purpose, and where basic core concepts of right and wrong no longer apply.

A society without strong, tough, masculine men is a society that is weak and complacent, one where children grow up without fathers, and where the basic concepts of protecting and providing are gone.

By the way, on the other side of this conversation here, femininity is also awesome. The world needs femininity. The world needs women, and it needs feminine women. I just wanted to make that point clear.

What is masculinity anyway?

Ask many people, and you'll get many answers. A big reason for this is that the concept of masculinity has been so beaten down in our society, and since it seems that you're not even supposed to like the idea of masculinity, you get mixed answers on the question in the first place.

Masculinity, in Western culture, has morphed into either just a personal opinion (different for every single person) or some unclear shapeless blob (a vague concept without any definition or purpose).

If we look at the media and the politically correct language used today, we run into the same issue as trying to figure out what a Real Man is. The media shows that a masculine man is supposed to be the uncaring macho man, and that he is all about beer, boobs, violence, sex, and so on. Or, on the other end of the spectrum, people will say that a masculine man is supposed to be basically a slightly less refined version of a feminine woman, that he is very emotional, and that must learn to control and put down his true nature.

Then people wonder why men are confused? Is this not obvious to everyone? Of course men are confused about manhood and masculinity, as is the rest of our society, when the word has been so redefined and diluted to be nearly meaningless to so many.

There is no fixed answer, just like in the prior chapter when I wrote about what a Real Man is, there is no one fixed box that all men will fit into. However, there are some common criteria.

Here is a great quote from Ted Dobson for you to consider,

"Unfortunately for themselves, their families, and their communities (men) have been satisfied with surface definitions of their masculinity, and have not probed the wonders of their deep masculine selves. Were they to choose to do so, our world would be a much different place, for men would be able to once again to truly lead, guide, and direct their own lives and others. They would be able to carry their fair share of the burdens of our human and Christian communities. They would once again be truly able to enjoy their lives, not in selfishness, but in the wonder of contributing their strength for the well–being of others."

I think that is a great definition: that a masculine man can lead, guide, and direct; that a masculine man will carry his fair share of burdens; and that he can again enjoy his life—in the wonder of contributing his strength for the well–being of others.

The strength and power of the masculine man comes from what he has inside, it comes from how he leads, how he inspires, how he follows his mission in life, how he is creating a legacy, how he is connecting with the people around him, how he is using his strength, and so on. Those are the true criteria of a masculine man.

Those are exactly the kind of significant men needed more in this world.

Twenty-Seven

THE TEAR IN THE MASCULINE SOUL

*I*t's no wonder men feel lost.

In the last chapter, I spoke some about the idea of masculinity itself. In this chapter, I'm going deeper, to the next level down. That next level is to an issue that is literally at the heart of all men—to the masculine soul itself.

Most men can feel the tear in their souls, even though most men can't really put that feeling into words or describe it in any clear terms to themselves, let alone to someone else. In this chapter, I'm going to try and help you to understand that feeling more, some of where it came from, and try to highlight some ideas about what you can do to help mend that tear.

For the vast majority of guys I speak with, as mentioned earlier, they have this inner pain, something that they can't really describe, something they can't put into words, something without reason or origin, something wrong that is just "there".

This is what I refer to as the *Tear in The Masculine Soul.*

As men, we were created with certain truths and certain realities, we were created with certain drives and certain callings, and we were created with certain needs and certain longings.

Over time however, we have learned to suppress most, if not all, of those. We deny our own reality, we deny our own calling, and we deny our own longings.

When was the last time you sat back and thought about this? When was the last time you planned and created something based on your own unique calling? When was the last time you built something, for you, based on your own passion and purpose? When was the last time you allowed yourself to explore your own needs and longings and thought about how to include them in your life?

If you're like I was, and are like most men who are reading this, the answer is never. We're not supposed to do that stuff. We're not supposed to want to do things that are masculine, we're not supposed to dig deeper into what it means to be a man (which is why I'm so grateful that you're reading this—because you've not fallen for those lies or you're waking up to them).

Without any complete picture of what it means to be a man, without any clear voices, without anywhere to turn in their own understanding of themselves as men, men find themselves left in the proverbial wilderness. There was, and there is, a void left about who men are supposed to be and who they are supposed to become.

Into that void came a whole bunch of new voices. You could just look at some book titles, magazine articles, or blog posts and see the trend as it grew: "Who Needs A Man Anyway?", "A Woman Needs A Man Like A Fish Needs A Bicycle", "Men Who Hate Women", "Men's War On Women", "Make Him Give You What You Want", "How To Be His Mother", and the list goes on and on...

Nearly everywhere you look, you can find another post, website, or book about how useless men are, about how women have no need for men, about how men need to be more like women, and this list also goes on and on...

It's no wonder that men feel lost. It is no wonder that men feel they have no place and no home in this society. Who feels like they have a home, when they are constantly told how unnecessary and unneeded they are in the first place? Who feels like they can have any peace, when they are constantly told that they're the source of all the problems in the world?

This leads men to retreating from whom they were created to be, retreating from their passions, callings, and longings, which in turn leads to the tear in their souls.

In a prior chapter, I used a quote from Ted Dobson, and I'm going to add another here. Mr. Dobson has written powerful words about these issues,

"Often they (men) are not active members of their own families, unable to have effective relationships with significant others, and unknowledgeable about how to rear their children. They often separate themselves from religion—that is, from developing a relationship with the center of the universe. They are often emotionally undeveloped, and their ability to care for and be care for is stunted. They often recoil from personal growth; many a counselor will report that in marriage difficulties the male rarely sees any problem in himself, that he refused to admit any responsibility for the problems, and that he especially refuses to change."

That, my brother, is the problem. The result of this problem is a man who has a tear in his soul. He is living, but he is not alive. He is without calling, without vision, without longing, and without purpose.

Men are often naturally attracted to the image of the lonely hero type of man, even though they know it is not fulfilling, deep down in their souls. One of the realities of that type of man is to be silent and distant, which usually causes a gap between boys and their own fathers, think back to the chapter about The Father Wound. In that gap is often what we find at the heart of the tear in the soul. A boy learns that a man is someone who is silent, someone who doesn't talk and share, and that a man is someone who remains distant.

This ends up affecting that boy's ability to grow on many levels, which then combined with society telling him that he isn't needed for anything... well the results we have today are clear.

As this tear becomes a bigger and bigger hole, it ends up affecting the core issues of who the man is, and opens him up to insecurity, to selfishness, to despair, and to depression.

We end up with men who struggle with these core issues of life, men who do not know who they are, men who do not know what it means to be a man, a father, a son, or a husband. Instead of using those core issues to define themselves and their roles in society, men end up basing their manhood on their stuff, the cars they own, the toys, the vacations, and all the other things that men can easily measure.

Now I know this has been a pretty serious message so far, there is lots here to think about, and I'm not just going to end here with the highlighting of a problem, because this all leads to the natural question, "OK, so now what do I do?"

Once we have realized that we have this tear, once we learn that our own fathers (and this isn't to put any blame on them, they did what they were taught as well) had and continue to have their own challenges, and we know that society isn't building up men, "Now what?" is the right question.

The answer starts with an acknowledgment. Acknowledge that this tear exists, like the Father Wound, and be open to the possibility that there is another way. Once you open your mind to the reality that the pain you're feeling is located deep down inside and that it is tied to your own identity as a man, you can start to see new opportunities and you can start to see life with a new set of eyes.

Here are some steps to consider:

- I suggest you commit to finding someone you can walk this walk with, someone who will have your back without judgment and who will be willing to tell you the truth when you are slipping off the path.
- I suggest that you be open and willing to enter into a relationship with God, who created you in the first place. If that statement causes you to pause, at least consider that perhaps that pause is reason enough to investigate further.
- I suggest you think about all the things you have heard about men, being a man, and masculinity, and think about how those things have shaped you and your own opinions of yourself over the years.
- I suggest you think about your own father, the good, the bad, and the ugly. What did you learn from him? What lessons did he teach you, even if they were unspoken? (Even men who grew up without their fathers end up learning lessons about fathers.)

Your job, as you are becoming a more significant man, is to redeem your own masculinity, and to heal this tear in your soul—and then to lead others around you on the same path. As with the other important issues in this series, this takes time and will not be easy, but is required of you as you continue to grow and experience more as a significant man.

Twenty-Eight
YOU ARE NOT A MISTAKE

Something I hear often is guys who think they are a mistake. Not that they have made a mistake, which we all have… no these are guys who think that they personally ARE the mistake. If you have ever thought that of yourself, you're not. Let's make that clear right here from the start.

You. Are. Not. A. Mistake.

A very common origin of this idea is something that Mom or Dad (or both) said to a young boy, and that has stuck with him his whole life. It might have sounded like these lines, which are all too familiar to so many men:

- Mom, "Getting pregnant with you was a mistake."
- Dad, "I wouldn't have married your mother if it wasn't for that one mistake that made you."
- Mom, "My life would have been so much easier if you were never around."
- Dad, "I wish you wouldn't have been born, so I could be free."

If you ever heard anything like that, it's very important for you to realize that neither of those statements are about you, even if they are said to you. They are statements about Mom and about Dad; they are statements that your Mom and Dad are saying about themselves, not about you.

By the way, if you've never heard anything like that, count your blessings. Those are not fictional lines to make a point; those are real lines that men have shared with me, over the years. Mothers and Fathers saying things like that is much more common than many realize.

Parents often say things like that in passing, in frustration, without even knowing what they are really saying. Yet that one throwaway line sticks with you for your entire life, eating away at you, instilling doubt about yourself over and over, becoming part of your story, all starting at an early age.

The parent often forgets that one line or quick comment, yet it is repeated again and again by the child, even continuing when the child is an adult. It becomes one of the self–fulfilling stories that gets repeated by the adult. Remember the chapter about your story; that chapter connects directly to this one.

This is why it is so critical that you, as a father, become aware of your own language and the things that you say to your own kids. Those "funny" lines might not be so funny to your son or daughter and might just be hurting them deeply for much of their lives.

Don't give them a story that they will have to work to re–write. Don't say things to them that they will later have to work to fix. Don't say things to them that you would not want your own parents to say to you. Make sure that you are not adding to any of the negative and disempowering stories that your kids will be telling.

It should come as no shock to you that your parents are human and they mess up just like everyone else. Parents screw up and they say things that they should not have said, and parents do things they should not have done.

Those things they've done and those words they've said are their screw ups, not yours. Those actions and words may have created wounds, and it is now time to let them heal, it is time to let those words go. You heard them, there is no pretending that never happened, but you have the ability to forgive and let them go. You have the choice to write a new story, you have the option to regain the power from those words of the past.

Today is when you can decide that your parent's words will no longer hurt you and no longer define you. Today is when you can take that power back.

The other common origin of this "I'm a Mistake" idea is self–imposed, over time. This one tends to come later in life and not to boys but rather to men. This is when men look back on the life they've lived so far, and feel like they have accomplished nothing. They feel that what they have to offer the world is nothing, and feel like they have made things worse than when they started. That feeling leads to the thought that they are a mistake and that the world would be better off if they were not around.

However, here is the thing: you are not a mistake. Period.

There is only one you on this entire planet. There has never been another you, and there will never be another you. Even if there happens to be someone else who looks identical to you, that person still isn't you.

You are the only you. Period.

You're the only one, in all of human history, with your talents, skills, personality, abilities, humor, emotions, and experiences. There is no one else who can fulfill the mission that you have been created to fulfill. No one else.

When God created you, He didn't make a mistake.

You have a mission. A calling. A longing. A purpose. What I have often found is that the feeling of being a mistake comes from not being in alignment with what you're currently doing and what you were created to do.

When what you do, especially in regards to your career, doesn't align with who you know you are, that causes problems. When you are not following your dream, and when you are not seeking to fulfill your calling, that causes more problems.

Those problems can make it seem like what you have now in life is a mistake, but do not confuse that with you being the mistake, because you are not.

You do need to go back to your dreams, back to your ideas, back to what made you come alive. And yes, you need to find a way to get that back into your life today.

The only mistake is that you're not yet living out the life that you were created to live, and you have the power to change that. You can choose to change.

Start using your power to make that change right now.

Twenty-Nine
YOU ARE NOT ALONE

When you're walking through this life, seeking more and trying to get better—better as a husband, better as a father, better as a man—there is a natural tendency to think that you are walking alone.

In general, men don't have many close friends that they can share life-changing journeys with, men tend to not have other men they can confide in, that they can trust, and that they can walk beside. And so men who are seeking more tend to feel alone.

This can especially be the case if you are unique, in what you are after, among your normal group of friends and family. When you are the only person who is trying to grow and change, who is trying to become more, and who is not satisfied or willing to accept the way things are, it can feel lonely.

Even more basic than that, the vast majority of men I work with tell me that they have this feeling of being alone when it comes to the serious stuff in their lives. They feel that they are going through their trials with no one who has their backs, and no one who lifts them when they fall.

Yes, these men, and probably you, have buddies, friends, and other people to go hang out with, to see a movie with, and to have fun with.

However, when it comes to the deep and real issues of life, most men feel… alone.

Here's the truth on this though. You're not alone. Although it is true that you may not yet have found the men who will walk beside you, who will support you, who will hold you accountable (in a good way), who will help you, and who will not judge you.

There are more men out there seeking what you are seeking than you know. There are men out there who want to be the kind of men who support their brothers going through the darkness, without judgement. There are men out there who want to learn as much as they can, about becoming a significant man, and lead others through the same process.

An awakening is taking place, where more and more men are seeing the possibility that there is more to life, and that they can live the life of a significant man. More and more men who want to become the heroes, warriors, and leaders that God created them to be.

What we all need, and this includes both you and me, is other men to walk the walk with us. You don't need the loud guys who only talk the talk, you need someone who sees the best in you, who wants to help bring it out, and who will be there for you. You need someone who sees what you are going through, and knows when to shut up and just be there for you.

All the junk and all the darkness in your life, no matter what it is, there is another man who has been there, who knows, who understands, and who can see it in your eyes with no words spoken.

All that pain that you think is only yours, the pain that you think no one else can comprehend, there is another man who has carried that same burden, faced those same demons, and felt the same shame, guilt, and darkness.

You're not alone.

I can't stress enough to you how important it is that you do the work needed to find at least one man who will be that man for you. This is a need that all men have, but few ever seek out and have in their lives.

Critically important here is to know that you cannot take this need to the woman in your life. If you take this need to the woman, you will find more pain and confusion, not solutions and steps for moving forward. Far too many good men and good women have ended up in a negative situation, where both wanted to do the right thing, but together it backfired. This is one place the feminine and masculine are not a perfect fit for one another. (To the ladies reading along, no disrespect here. We love you, but this is sort of thing is where a man needs another man to have his back.)

Here is how you can know if you have this sort of man in your corner. If your life imploded tomorrow, your marriage was going downhill, your financial situation was tanking, you couldn't talk to your kids, or you were battling serious depression; in other words if those very real and very serious things were happening, who would you call? Who exactly would you talk to?

The vast majority of men do not have even one name to put to those questions. You might have the guys to talk about cars and movies with, but a man to talk to about sex and intimacy challenges? No chance. What about someone to talk with about how you and your wife aren't getting along anymore? Nope, not going to happen. What about someone to talk with about how porn is damaging your relationship? No one come to mind yet?

That's exactly the challenge, and exactly the truth for most guys, so don't feel bad if you didn't have one single name come to mind either.

Remember as you start working through this issue: You are not alone; there are men who understand and there are men who will have your back. You may have to work to find them, you may find them at the events I lead with the Significant Man, you may find them in your community, your church, your work, your gym, or your gun club, but they are there.

It is your job to do this, you have to be willing to go through the process of finding them. Once you do, you will have claimed a new source of power on your journey.

As I wrap up this chapter, think about these words from Ecclesiastes, "Two are better than one, because they have a good return for their work: If one falls down, his friend can help him up. But pity the man who falls and has no one to help him up! ...Though one may be overpowered, two can defend themselves."

Thirty

YOUR CHANGE IS A THREAT

In the last chapter, I made a comment about how your changes can feel lonely if you're the only one you know who is changing. I'm going to expand on this concept here, as it is a very important issue that needs some more time.

I hear this sort of thing from the men I work with: "Warren, how come it seems that as I am making all these changes, as I am trying harder and harder to become better, to really become that significant man I have inside, it seems like the most resistance comes from people I know and love? Why would that be where so many of the challenges come from?"

I understand this question; I've felt those same challenges and that same resistance. If you have as well, you know that it really hurts. The reason that it hurts, the reason that those comments and questions seem to be such a bother, is that they hit us right in the gut as men. We expect strangers to have those comments, but not people who are close to us and whom we love. We're prepared to dodge and deal with such comments from strangers, but we are not prepared to hear them from those who are close.

I've had men tell me about hearing comments like these:

- "This is all a waste of your time, nothing is going to change."
- "Why would you spend money on mentoring, when you know it is just a scam?"
- "You don't need anything like that, you are already where you should be."
- "What a joke, how weak are you to need that?"
- "Just be a man already."

And on and on. Usually you'll hear the comments directly, but sometimes they come to you through someone else. That someone else is often your wife, meaning that someone comments to her about you and what you are doing. That puts her in an awful position, and if that is happening to her, you need to understand she is now in that position. You need to support her 100% as she is dealing with those side comments.

As you are evolving, as you continue on your journey towards becoming a more significant man, you will run into this more and more until you have crossed the line and everyone knows you are serious and can see that you have made it.

There are multiple reasons for this resistance, however it would take us a long discussion to really dig deep on all of them, so I'll stick to one of the biggest high level reasons here:

You change is a threat. That's it. It's as simple as that.

Your change is a threat to the status quo, no matter how good or bad it might be today. Your change is a threat that relationships will change. Your change is a threat that economics will change. Your change is a threat that you will connect with God, maybe for the first time. Your change is a threat to the safety and security of the current situation, and people don't like that.

What is often the biggest threat is that your changes shine a massive billion-watt spotlight on the fact that change really is possible. If you do it, then they should also be able to, which is where the real threat is located.

You making new tough choices, you thinking about and taking action on new things, you changing, you becoming more, you doing what you need to do shows that changing really can be done, and it shows that there is no reason to accept the current reality as the future reality.

Change is often quite uncomfortable, and people don't like that. Most people want to continue with how things are today; they don't really want things to be different tomorrow. Most people are content to continue with how their lives are today (even if their lives aren't great) than they are committed to doing anything about making new choices, making changes, and making a new life.

However, when you change, when you show the results, when you become that man you were created to become, suddenly they are aware of their current reality.

What's important to realize here is that they are not even talking about you. All those comments, looks, and eye rolls, those are all really about them, their pain, their dissatisfaction, their frustration, their wounds, and their own lives. It's not about you, it's about them.

They are more upset over the fact that they have not made any changes than they are over the fact that you have. You just happen to be easier to "lash out" towards than their own reflection in the mirror is. Their anger or confusion is often simply because you have opened a wound (likely unintentionally) and now they are forced, even for a brief moment, to confront their wound.

A simple example of this is when someone, who is overweight and has overweight friends, chooses to do the work and make the changes to get into a healthier shape. Quite often, this person, who is now in better shape, will receive angry looks, annoyed attitudes, and sarcastic comments from their friends who are still overweight. Those looks, comments, and attitudes might be directed towards you, if you are the one who lost weight, but they are really about the internal wound that the overweight person is still feeling.

Your changes, your choices, those all show what can be done, and that is threatening to someone who isn't willing or ready to make any changes or tough choices for themselves. So it becomes much easier to hold you back, so to speak, than it does to support and encourage you to become more. The threat is real to them, even if they haven't thought it through to this level.

Unfortunately, just as no one else can do your work for you, you can't make them understand until they are ready to see the possibilities for themselves.

Often the harder you push and try to convince others about what you are doing, the greater the resistance becomes.

That doesn't mean you shouldn't tell anyone what you're doing, but it does mean you shouldn't expend your energy trying to sell someone on your change when they aren't ready to hear it and are going to become a blockade on your path. Instead, be a positive example.

Be encouraging if and when they ask what you're doing; but don't push anything on them as they are walking their own journey. When they are ready, and they see what you have done, do not be surprised if they open up and wish to join you where you are.

When they get there, give them a warm smile, a big hug, and welcome them to the next level.

Thirty-One

YOUR BATTLE PLAN

*E*ven after talking with men about these big issues for decades it still surprises me how few men have a strategy for their own lives. Men have plans and strategies for their jobs, they have plans and strategies for the work they do, they have plans and strategies for their hobbies and projects, but they don't have plans and strategies for their lives.

Lots of guys will have spent more time on the strategy for their fantasy football league than they will have spent on the strategy for their own real life.

That's just crazy.

If you're going to drive from Miami to Seattle, you have a plan. If you're going to take a vacation, you have a plan. If you're going out for a date night (which you better be guys, you better be), you have a plan. Even if your plans don't detail every step, you still have some sort of plan.

But most men, for their actual life? They're just going along day–by–day, instead of following any sort of plan at all.

Does that mean you have to have a specific strategy and plan for every little detail of your life? Of course not, there is no need to get down to that level. That's not even a good idea, really. Few men will do well making the shift from no plan at all to micromanaging every aspect of their own lives, so don't go to the other extreme.

But at least have a plan!

- How exactly are you planning to change your financial situation?
- How specifically are you planning to make an impact in your relationship with your wife?
- How exactly are you planning to become a better father to your children?
- How specifically are you planning to get into better shape?
- How exactly are you planning to create that connection to God?

Note: As you're reading this, keep it in context with the chapter about The Incredible Power of Your Why. You need to have the powerful Why behind your changes, before you focus energy on the How. What I'm sharing in this chapter is what you do after you have that Why in place—in other words once you know why, then you get to work on the how.

If you have no plan, no strategy at all, that means you're just wishing and hoping that somehow something good might happen someday. That's it, nothing more. The change you say you want isn't actually real; you might like the idea of change, you might enjoy thinking about becoming a more significant man, but that's as far as you're willing to go.

Because without a strategy in place, the odds of you getting where you want to go are pretty much zero. Wishful thinking doesn't get you there. Hoping isn't going to change your situation.

If you are the coach of a football team, do you create a strategy for the next game? Do you get your best players lined up in the right positions? Or do you just tell them to make it up, all on their own, and hope for the best? Of course not, you would have a specific plan of attack to win the game.

Just like the football game, you need a strategy to execute, for your life; you need a plan to implement. Take some time, after you are done with this chapter today, and really think about this.

While micromanaging isn't what you need, a plan is. So write down, as in good old fashioned pen and paper, time in your schedule (and yes you do have the time) for you to spend on where you are going to take your life, and start to detail out the how you're going to get there.

Plan each day to learn and expand your mind. Reading books and chapters like this one is a great start. Plan each day to work on your financial situation. Skip the TV show, do less web surfing, and get to work on your finances.

Plan each day to build the relationship between you and your wife. Pick a time to call her, text her, or email her, every single day. Plan each day to connect with God. Pray, read, study, watch a video, or whatever works for you, get it in your daily strategy.

Plan each day to get into better shape. If you don't have a place to start then go for a walk, jog, run, or anything else that you can start today without a massive time or financial investment, get that into your schedule for every day.

Once you have created your plan, then transfer that to an actual document you can use to keep track of how you are doing. Create a simple checklist for every day of the week, and note your progress.

This is more than just a discussion about time management. Yes, you need to set aside the time to do these things, but where the change takes place is in what you do during those times. After you have the time planned into your schedule, then be specific on what you are doing at those times. Have specific and exact things you are going to do during that time. Plan it ahead of time, and execute your plan.

Building the habit of working your plan is critical, realizing that it's much more than a plan. This is you, being on offense, making the choice to take specific action and do specific work. Instead of just hoping for change, instead of just dreaming that things might be different someday, this is your specific method you use to make that dream become reality.

So create your strategy and execute it just like you would a battle plan—because that is what it actually is. This is the battle plan for your life. You are at war, but in this war you get to decide the outcome, you get to create the plan and you get to create the outcome you desire.

Every day take a step forward on each part of your strategy. Every day fight for your future. Every day fight for your strategy, and keep on fighting until you are on your path to victory.

Thirty-Two
WHY DO MEN LIKE THOSE MOVIES?

*I*t seems like a simple question, and it seems like it might have a simple answer, but it doesn't.

The question is, "Why do men love movies like Braveheart, Gladiator, and James Bond?"

Often I hear that it is because of the violence, the swords/guns/weapons, the explosions, and so on. Yes, to a degree, that may be a part of it, but there is so much more beyond that. What is under the violence that attracts men? Because, there have been many violent movies that are disliked and quickly forgotten.

As men, we are seeking something. We have a need, a longing, and a desire that is almost impossible for most of us to put into words. Often, when we do try to put it into words, those words come out in a jumbled mess, so we don't try again.

Outside of possibly our own fathers, or the man who functioned as our father, most men really do not have any real role models of how to be a man. As a part of this issue, we look to the lead character in those movies for an example, an idea, or a vision, of what a man actually is.

However, we're not looking at them as most people think we are. We're not looking at them as being the ultra-macho guy and wishing we were too, we're not looking at them as being in perfect shape and thinking we should be too, and we're not looking at them as always getting new ladies and wishing we did too… it isn't about being a macho man with both guns blazing.

It is not those surface issues. While that does work on movie posters and commercials, that is not what the real deeper draw to men is, because we don't have those issues in common.

In fact, we don't actually have much in common with the lead characters at all. And that is where the draw comes from, that is what is at the core of why us men love these movies so much, it is what takes place under all the stuff that is going on, on the surface.

For most of us guys, we have very deeply rooted needs, and those needs do not have an outlet and do not have a place to exist in most of modern society. If you ask the average man what he needs or what it means to be a man, he will not be able to answer the question with any clarity or certainty.

The reality is that we know we have these questions, and that they that are tied into our souls, but we also know that we don't have a means of expressing them. Since our words so often seem to fail us, and we have such a hard time identifying the needs ourselves, we revisit these movies—movies that connect with the deep parts of ourselves—parts we have a hard time discussing.

As men, we long for a battle to win. Not a war, not taking over a country or stopping the evil guy from ruling the world, but a battle. We need a battle to fight and a battle to win.

But it isn't just a fight for the sake of a fight. That is what much of society gets wrong. It isn't fighting simply to fight, that is not what men are seeking.

It is a fight with a purpose, not just a fight. It is a battle that matters. And how do we most often define what that purpose is and what matters? We define it with the woman we love. Woman. Singular.

As men, we long for any chance to be the hero to her. We need to know we can become that man, when called upon. Almost anything will do. If we are driving and the car gets a flat tire, we have to get out there and change it, fast.

If it happens to be raining, with hail and lightning and maybe even a tornado on the way, that makes changing the tire all that much better. We need to ensure our family is safe and that, even for that one brief moment, we know that we have what it takes.

As men, we also long for an adventure. As with the chance to be the hero, and like being the hero, almost anything will do when it comes to the longing for adventure. We need to have ourselves tested, to be doing something that we might consider dangerous (gasp!), something on the edge that is beyond the safety of our current lives.

When we are on an adventure, we feel more alive than we can describe. We also might be scared, we might be physically hurting, we might be confused, we might even be terrified, but we will be *alive*.

Now think about the lives of most men.

Is there a battle to fight? Not even close. For most men, the main battle is getting through a week of work without an incident. If somehow we do happen to get into a battle, we're told we shouldn't have. Starting as boys, we are told to sit down, to be quiet, to not fight, and that continues to be what we hear as we age, so there is no battle in our lives anymore.

Is there an opportunity to be a hero? Rarely, if ever. For most men, the main chance at being a hero is getting rid of a bug in the house. Which we'll do, because at this point we'll take anything over nothing.

Is there adventure in their lives? Almost never. Think of all the men you know, when was the last real adventure for any of them? Most men have to go back to their own childhood to find even one example of an adventure.

So you see, these movies allow us to connect with something much deeper than all the surface issues, they allow us to connect with our core needs, as men, and allow us just a glimpse of what we are seeking in our lives.

To the ladies who are reading along, and thank you again for wanting to get this glimpse into the minds of men. If you are with a good man, then know this:

- He needs a battle to fight and what he really wants to fight for is you. More than anything he wants to fight for you, so please don't stop him from doing so.
- He needs to be a hero. Let him. If he can be a hero while serving or protecting you, all the better, so please don't stop him from this either.

- He needs to have adventure in his life. Encourage him, don't discourage him. Yes, it might be dangerous and yes, there is risk—that's the entire point!

So men, my friends, get into the battle, become the hero, and live an adventure.

Note: This chapter (like much of this book) is directly inspired from the work of John Eldredge and his book, *Wild at Heart*, which I highly recommend you read.

Thirty-Three
SHE STOOD UP

There are many movies that men love, and there are many reasons why, in the prior chapter I shared some of the reasons why men love Gladiator, James Bond, and Braveheart. Today we're going to talk about a specific movie scene which is incredibly powerful for totally different reasons.

In the film, The Natural, there is a short scene which has brought countless men to tears. For my fellow men, this chapter might explain why this scene moves you so much, and for the ladies this is an important one for you to realize. I can't emphasize enough how important this is.

The hero of the movie, Roy Hobbs, is a professional baseball player who has been struggling. He has a yearning deep in his soul, but his career is not working out the way he wanted. He is up to bat and the entire world seems to be against him.

The crowd is jeering him. The announcers are talking about his career being over. Even his own teammates and his own coach are looking at him with negativity. No one believes in him. No one trusts that he can play anymore. It really looks like the end for him, and it isn't going to end well.

He swings once and misses, strike one. He swings again, and again he misses, strike two. Then something happens. Please go watch this short clip (yes, please go type this into a web browser or click if you're reading this electronically), and then we'll continue…

https://youtu.be/J0lof7tFKtE

In one brief moment, everything changed. It is that moment which brings tears to the eyes of so many men (in addition to the great movie itself and powerful soundtrack). Did you catch the moment; did you see what really happened?

When it looked as if he was done and that no one believed in him: one person was willing to stand up. And it happened to be the one person he needed to stand up: it was, her.

- She stood up, alone, in the middle of the crowd.
- She stood up, alone, in the middle of the jeering.
- She stood up, alone, when no one else would.

She did not stand up and yell his name. She did not stand up and try to correct or shout back at the crowd.

She did not stand up and tell him how to hold the bat. She did not stand up and tell him how to swing. She did not stand up and tell him how to watch for the next pitch. She did not tell him anything she thought he was supposed to do.

She simply stood up for him. For. Him.

In doing so, she told him, "I stand with you. I stand behind you. I stand beside you. I stand with you no matter what happens." Most importantly, she told him, "I believe in you. I believe in what you are doing. I believe in what you will do. I will always be on your side, even when no one else is."

Yes, it was a brief moment, just a glimpse, but that moment, when everything was on the line and when it seemed that no one else in the world was on his side, that glimpse said everything.

That is one reason why, in the context of this scene, this movie means so much to men, and why this one particular scene moves men so deeply.

Men crave that sort of thing from the woman they love; they yearn for it in their souls.

Because as men we have a longing in our souls to matter, to be someone, to become a hero, and most of all to become a hero to the woman in our lives. Yes, we want to be the hero to our sons and daughters, but most of all is to be the hero to our wives.

Any chance will do. As I mentioned in the prior chapter, from getting rid of a bug in the house or changing a flat tire in the rain, to hitting a home run, and we want to take that chance. Any opportunity to be the hero, even if just for a brief moment in time, and we want to become that hero.

When we are down on our luck, when it seems the entire world is against us, if that one woman in our lives will just stand up with us, then it doesn't matter who is against us. After all, the most important person on the planet is for us!

Guys, this is why her lack of support hurts so much. Because deep down in your soul you know that she is the single person who knows you better than anyone else on Earth. And if she doesn't support you or your work, and she's the one who knows you the best, then you think (even if on a subconscious level) that she must be right, and you don't follow through.

However, on the other hand, when she is by your side, when she is standing up—for you—nothing, and I mean nothing, can stop you from reaching your goal. You won't even stop yourself in that situation, because you know that you are on the path to becoming the hero you have inside. It won't matter if all the other billions of people on Earth don't believe in you, if she does, you will find a way.

Let her encourage you, let her believe in you, let her stand up for you. Let her use her amazing feminine power for you. You will find strength you never knew you had inside when she does.

Ladies if you've read along with this chapter, I hope this has given you a different perspective into this issue, and perhaps another look into the incredible power you have, with your man.

If you have a good man, one who loves you and who respects you, you standing up for him, even when (and especially when) he doesn't believe in himself anymore, can change his entire world.

You standing up can be the difference between his third strike or his home run.

So please, stand up!

Thirty-Four

YOU NEED AN ADVENTURE

Here is a question that many men don't want to hear. Not necessarily because they can't answer it, but because they can and the answer isn't one they want to admit:

When was your last real adventure?

Yep, I thought so. If you say it has been a long time, or maybe you even say you have never had an adventure, then you know the problem already, even if you can't really articulate it.

Let's get right to the point: as a man you need an adventure, you need a battle, you need risk and danger in your life, something I talk about quite a bit with the men I mentor and have mentioned already in this book. If you're feeling empty, dull, and bored inside, odds are nearly 100% that you don't have that adventure anywhere—there is exactly zero adventure in your life.

You need some.

Go find it, and experience something you have been sorely missing, experience something that you desperately need to experience.

I do not consider this an option, by the way. Men need adventure. When we are younger, this came much more easily and without much thought. As we get older and we get consumed with life and responsibility soon the very idea of adventure seems like something that should be left to the younger men, left to those without families, left to those without the health issues, left to those without the business to look after, and so on.

Without adventure however, there is a big piece of a man's soul that is missing. Men were born for adventure; they were born to battle and take risks.

By the way, this doesn't mean you go give up your common sense and do something stupid! It doesn't mean you decide to go and try skydiving without a parachute, hoping to catch up and tandem with another jumper who has a spare. You can have adventure and you can take risks without being a completely reckless idiot at the same time.

Show me a room of 50 men who are bored and dull, and I can guarantee you that those 50 men do not have any adventure in their lives even if they have met all the popular means of success. Those bored and dull men have bought the Ferrari (which is awesome) and have never driven it over the speed limit. Those are the men who have the means to travel anywhere in the world, but will never leave the comfort and safety of their Five–Star all–inclusive resorts (which are awesome). Those are the men who have all the best ski gear (which is awesome), but never consider hitting a slope that they can't already safely ski down.

In other words, even if a man has the big house, the great cars, the money, and all of that, if there is no actual adventure or risk in his life, there is a part of that man who has been numbed down inside.

You might not have realized that is what is at the core of the empty feeling, but when you start to think about it, you'll soon realize the truth in this reality. This lack of adventure directly leads to blandness in a man's life.

When a man tells me about his last adventure, I can see him light up. His chest comes out, his shoulders go back, and his voice gets stronger, even if just on a subtle level. Internally, his pulse quickens, his eyes get a bit larger, and some of that energy and enthusiasm he felt as a boy starts to return.

I have yet to hear a man tell me about an adventure he had that wasn't dangerous to some degree, where he almost died, where he almost lost a limb, where the weather was impossible, where the odds were against him, or where he wasn't sure he would get home… you get the idea.

When he does tell me about this experience he has had, I know that he will be happy, energized, and excited. Isn't that odd? He'll be talking about a situation where he nearly died, where he was lost in the wilderness, or where he thought he wasn't going to make it, and then tell me this was one of the greatest moments of his life?

Actually no, there is nothing odd about that at all, and as a man, you instinctively know this. Because, in our guts we know that we're supposed to experience adventure. And we'll remember our adventures, even if they are from years or decades in the past.

That man telling me about his adventure will literally change emotionally and physically while he is retelling the story of his adventure. And, this is just from the mere mention of him telling me about his last adventure from years gone by… imagine if he actually has another one now. Imagine if you have one now!

Guys, this really isn't something you can consider to be an option for "someday". Yes, I am aware that scheduling your adventure is something that you will have to work out with your wife, with your work, and with the kid's school schedules, but you need to work through the logistics. You need to be willing to go to bat for yourself. After all, are you really the kind of guy who is willing to give up on adventure because it wasn't easy to fit into your schedule? Are you sure you want to live with that? Don't choose to let this go because it took some work to make it happen.

Remember the earlier chapter about the need for you to have a battle plan for your life? Well, including some adventure in that plan is critical. This means that when you are going through your planning, when you are making time for yourself, add an adventure to what you are creating.

Find your adventure, whatever it happens to be, and take that risk. You will come alive and you will become energized in a way you might not even remember you had inside.

Think about this famous newspaper ad, from 1914. This was from Ernest Shackleton, looking for men to join him on his South Pole Expedition:

"MEN WANTED for hazardous journey, small wages, bitter cold, long months of complete darkness, constant danger, safe return doubtful, honor and recognition in case of success."

He received over 5,000 applicants! Let that sink in. Over 5,000 men responded to that ad. Because that ad speaks right into the need for adventure we have as men. I'm willing to bet that ad still stirs something in your own soul as you read it today, more than 100 years later.

You need adventure. It's time to start experiencing life, and to live an adventure, for you.

Thirty-Five
THAT ANNOYING VOICE

You know the voice, because you've heard it your whole life. It seems like you always hear it at the worst possible times, like during major decisions, while you are starting a project, or when you are finally working on your dream.

Sometimes it is a quiet voice, just whispering in the back of your mind. At other times though the voice is screaming so loudly that you cannot hear or think of anything other than what the voice is yelling at you.

You know the voice, but do you listen to the questions:

- "When are you going to grow up?"
- "Why are you doing this?"
- "Who do you think you are?"
- "Why would God care about you?"
- "What do you have to offer anyone?"
- "Why would your business succeed?"

You know the voice, but do you listen to the statements:

- "You'll never make it."
- "You'll never be good enough."
- "You'll never find love."
- "You'll never earn real money."
- "You'll never become significant."

You know the voice, but do you listen to the conclusions:

- "Just give up now."
- "Time to stop following your dream."
- "No one will ever listen to you."
- "Play it small and safe instead."

We all have this voice. You do. I do. Everyone you know does. Some will admit it, others will run away from it, and others will pretend they do not have such a voice.

If you want to become a significant man, you need to confront this voice. You need to acknowledge that it exists, and then you get to work.

Recall that earlier I mentioned that you are in the Battle of Your Life. This voice is the main tool of your enemy in that battle.

This voice has been working on you for your entire life. The voice is the accumulation of a lifetime of what you have already heard and thought. It knows your deepest and darkest fears, and it loves to use that knowledge against you, at just the right time, to hold you back.

Perhaps when you were young your Mom got upset at you when you asked for something, and so you learned that you shouldn't be asking for things. What you never knew was that she was stressed and worried and her getting upset at you actually had nothing to do with what you asked for. Yet, a small little voice started to grow telling you that when you ask for things, that is bad; so now you hear that voice telling you that you shouldn't ask for anything.

Perhaps a lifetime of rules about what life is and is not supposed to be have given power to the voice.

You have heard that "All men are…" or that "All fathers should…" or that "All husbands are supposed to…" so what happens if you don't fit into one of those categories?

You start to question, you start to pull back in, and you start to reconsider what you have been doing and what you are going to do next. You start wondering if you'll ever do anything right and wondering if you'll ever be a good husband or father. All of this ends up hitting you really deeply, as a man. This isn't superficial questioning about where to go for dinner, this is going right to your core. These questions are about who you are.

So what do you do? How do you deal with this voice?

First, recognize it. That awareness is critical. Don't pretend that this voice doesn't exist for you.

Second, become aware that this voice has been building up over your whole life, and that this voice has been collecting words and stories to repeat to you since you were born. The voice has been fed by all the people in your life, and it loves to get louder at just the wrong times for you.

Third, understand that the world has an idea about your life, and that idea will almost never align with your own idea. Understand that God has an idea about your life, and that might not align with your own dreams either.

Lastly, and perhaps most importantly, realize that this world has an enemy, an enemy who loves to get into your head and lie to you. This enemy loves to create confusion and pain in your thoughts. The enemy of this world uses that little voice to cause you to question, to doubt, and to stop your pursuit of your dreams. The enemy of this world wants to make sure that you never do the things you were created to do.

Learn to hear this voice differently from your genuine thoughts. You know what your hopes, dreams, and longings are, and you know when you are in alignment with them. You'll recognize that annoying voice because it is bringing you down, it is making you question, and it is making you doubt.

Make it your goal to identify this voice quickly, to notice when it starts creeping into your awareness, and learn to stop that voice from taking hold in your mind.

When you do start taking action like this, when you do start to really follow your calling and use your gifts, you will find that little voice losing power. It will never disappear, but you can learn to recognize it quickly, understand it is a distraction, and you can learn not to listen to the lies.

When you do, you have taken back your own power, and you will experience a new level of peace and accomplishment.

Thirty-Six

A COURAGEOUS MAN

Have courage men, have courage.

Lines like that tend to create deep emotional responses in men. We love courage. We love the ideas that come into our minds when we think of courage. Why is that? How could five simple words end up meaning so much?

Let's start first with trying to understand what courage is to begin with. When you think about courage, what do you think of? What images or visions come to mind?

Normally, men think of a soldier in battle, doing something heroic and dangerous. Men think of an act of bravery that could result in the loss of life or limb. Men think of David defeating Goliath. Men think of a man, out in the woods, fighting a wolf with his bare hands. Men think of great men doing great things. Doing. Taking action.

This means that men equate courage to action, and they should. It is hard to be courageous without action. Sitting at home watching another TV show requires no courage. Sitting at home playing another video game requires no courage. Sitting at home while your wife raises your children requires no courage.

Therefore, courage requires action, and men love action.

Sometimes however, these standard definitions of courage leave us regular men feeling like we are lacking courage in our own lives. After all, I'm not fighting in the Army, the Marines, the Air Force, or any other area of military service, so is there courage in my life? I'm not hanging from a helicopter, rescuing a climber down in a canyon. I'm not a firefighter running into a burning building.

Am I courageous then? Can I even be courageous without any of those things?

Yes, I can and yes, you can. In order to realize how, we need to reframe our understanding of courage somewhat. While all those things absolutely require courage and are courageous actions, they are the start of the courage list—not the end of it.

When you sit back and think of the men you consider courageous and you ask them about their work, few of them would tell you that they were courageous. Few would start with, "Remember that time I was so totally awesome and courageous? Yeah, that was great."

No, they wouldn't say that. Instead, they would likely minimize what they have done, likely seek somewhere else for the spotlight, and likely seek another person to take the conversation.

What they would say is that they were doing their jobs. They would say they were doing what they were trained to do. They would say they were following through and doing the right thing. And all were doing so without regard for their own outcome.

When the firefighter runs into the burning building, when the soldier runs towards the sound of gunfire, he is not doing that in order to become a hero or to demonstrate just how much courage he has.

He is doing his job. He is doing what he is called to do.

There we are again, back to action. Back to doing.

For you and me, as we go through our lives, probably without ever having to run into a burning building, how do we show and demonstrate courage? How do we incorporate courage into our life?

The truth is that we have opportunities to be courageous every day, and most of us actually are being courageous every day. But, we don't think we are, because we are stuck in the "burning buildings and gunfire" definition of courage.

In reality, courage is doing what we know is right, even when we don't want to. Most men will quit, most men will give up, most men will retreat into their fortress instead of doing what they know is right.

Courage can mean that you got up, out of bed, and went to work, when you didn't want to. You know that it is your duty to provide for your family, and so you do what you have to do, even on those days when you would rather stay under the covers.

Courage can mean that you stopped being a playmate with your kids, and you disciplined them, when you didn't want to. Most of us dads would much rather just play and have fun with our kids than be the disciplinarian, but there are times our children and wives need us to be that man.

Courage can mean that you had the difficult conversation with your wife, when you didn't want to. You know that one important conversation that you have been avoiding; it can take a tremendous amount of courage to have that talk.

In other words, courage is doing what is right, when it isn't easy to. Courage is you taking action on something you know you need to take action on, even though you don't want to.

Those are some of the ways that men can demonstrate courage to themselves, their wives, and their children.

Notice that real courage can take many different forms, and all of them are valid. And notice that real courage is rooted in doing, it is rooted in action.

If you make the choice to take action, if you choose to do what is right, even when you don't want to, then you are a courageous man.

Thirty-Seven
YOUR STRUGGLE ISN'T YOUR IDENTITY

You'll see this quote "Your Struggle Isn't Your Identity" on social media, from time to time, and it is a good one; I use it myself. But it needs some explanation as the quote alone is only interesting, only an idea without definition.

What does it really mean?

Well, in order to explain this you need to step back and consider two primary concepts. First, what is your current struggle? And second, what is your current identity?

Because if you cannot clearly define what those are, you are living in a cloudy area of confusion and fog—fog which has stayed around you for a long time with no sign of lifting. So that is where we are going to start with this.

What is your true struggle? Really, what is it?

It will be different for each of us; so consider these questions, based on struggles that men have shared with me over the years: Are you condescending? Are you mean spirited? Are you broken? Are you lost? Are you ego-driven? Are you inconsiderate? Are you afraid? Are you unloving? Are you helpless? Are you a failure? Are you blaming others for your reality? Are you addicted to porn?

Are you depressed? Are you angry? Are you worried you will never earn enough money? Are you pride-filled?

As you start to think about those questions, I'm sure your own questions and struggles will start to come to the surface. It may take some time, but you know in your soul what your struggle is.

Now as you think about that struggle, how has it become associated with your identity? Or worse, has that struggle actually become your identity?

Like above then, we need to examine and understand what your identity actually is, so what is your identity? What kind of man are you? Here are some other questions for you to think about:

Are you the kind of man who pulls others down? Are you the man who hides behind a happy mask? Are you the man who is arrogant? Are you the man who rains down the storm on others? Are you the man who feels like he is never good enough?

Before I move on, I want to add a personal note here…

This subject is a personal one to me, as I was the textbook example of this exact issue. For a long time, well beyond a few years, I was in this situation. My struggle was in figuring out what I was supposed to do, and wearing the burden of prior failures (including what those failures meant to me and to my family).

I got stuck in looking at every one of the puzzle pieces, instead of just putting the puzzle together. It became part of my identity. I became "an entrepreneur who had lost everything" and said that I "didn't know what to do next to take care of my family".

That struggle itself became my identity, and the weight of it was overwhelming. Every day I felt the weight of that struggle and identity on my back, every minute I was awake it was there, every conversation it was there. I carried the weight of being a failure every second of every day, and it was a crushing weight. I would shed tears in the shower about how I was letting everyone down. I would even have dreams (more like nightmares) about how I lost it all, how I was not doing what everyone else told me I "should be" doing, and how I would lose it again. So yes, I had this issue deeply ingrained into me.

The irony is that I teach how we cannot let our income, our career, our possessions, etc… how we cannot let any of that become our identity, how we cannot let that define who we are. Yet, prior to all of this work myself, I had been the worst offender of this issue.

Something I had vowed I would never do became exactly what I was doing!

The benefit now is that I can see this quickly in others and can help people through this, and had I not gone through that, at such a deep, personal, and painful, level myself I would not be able to help others through this as I do now.

As you are thinking about this, there is a simple statement I want you never to forget, "You are not what broke you."

In other words, you are not the problem you are facing, you are not the challenge in front of you, and you are most definitely not the struggle you are about to overcome.

When you hear yourself start to use this phrase, "I am …" pay more attention to the words that follow than to any words you have ever paid attention to before. What you say, following the words "I am" will have incredible power over your entire life. Incredible power.

Anytime you start to hear yourself saying (including in your own mind to yourself) something that directly associates your struggle to your identity, you need to stop. Literally, stop. Do not allow yourself to finish the sentence.

Change the "I am" sentence from one about your struggle to one about your power, your purpose, your potential, and your strength. This is how you rewrite your story, as mentioned earlier in this book.

You need to understand that you are in the middle of one of the most epic battles of your entire life.

This battle over your identify and your struggle is one of the great battles that will define your life, this battle will shape your legacy and your impact on future generations. How you choose to define yourself, how you describe your identity has incredible power over who you actually are.

You are at war. It is the war for your very soul and your very meaning as a man on this planet. I've mentioned this before, this battle you are in, and this is one of the front lines in that fight.

To work through this issue, which you need to do, I want you to step back and consider the three things:

First, clearly identify what your current struggle really is. (You have to be honest here)

Second, clearly define what your current identity is. (Don't judge yourself, just define here)

Third, clearly list what words you use when you say, "I am…" (Be ruthlessly truthful here)

Then take those pieces of information and get to work on your battle plan. You have to be honest and true here, otherwise this will continue to be a disempowering aspect of your life. Clearly know yourself and clearly attack this issue with intention.

Refuse to use the negative "I am…" language anymore and replace it with something powerful. Even if you don't fully believe it yet, do not allow yourself to speak the negative phrase anymore, do not give any more power to those negative stories.

If you continue to empower your negative statements about yourself, you will experience a life filled with that negativity. Instead, if you choose to empower your positive statements about yourself, then you will experience a life filled with positivity. You get to choose.

You can choose to take back your power from the struggle. You can choose to create a new identity. You have the ability to do that, starting today.

And never forget, "You are not what broke you."

Thirty-Eight
NICE GUYS DON'T FINISH LAST (EVER!)

You've heard the saying "Nice Guys Finish Last" forever, you might have said it yourself; maybe even to yourself when you look in the mirror. But, here is the thing… it's a lie. Nice guys don't finish last. Ever!

Ready for the gut punch? Here it is:

Nice guys are far too average and unremarkable to do enough to finish last. Nice guys will never risk enough to come in last, and they will never risk enough to come in first.

Nice guys will be content to finish somewhere in the middle, somewhere that nobody notices, somewhere that has no impact on the outcome at all.

A nice guy will never use his talents all the way, he will never step out into that uncomfortable place where he could go farther.

Nice guys live in the world of safe. Nice guys fear either end of the spectrum; coming in first would bring an unwanted spotlight while coming in last would bring judgment and discontent.

So they stay in the middle, never rocking the boat, never causing a fuss, never getting out of line.

Men today are hurting, and much of that pain comes back to this issue of being nice. Men feel like they have to be nice, they have to be calm, they have to be pleasant, and that they have to hide their true nature inside.

Therefore, out of fear that the real man underneath might be seen and exposed, there is a mask of nice always being worn by the man. The nice guy is an illusion, a mask, a cover of the reality of who he is, as a man. For many nice guys, they will wear this mask to their graves.

If you are a nice guy, you know this place well. And, odds are very high that you hate it.

For the nice guy to move out of this place, the place he hates, he is going to have to choose to do things differently than he has done before, maybe ever before in his entire life.

This is an extremely challenging position for the nice guy. He knows he can be doing so much more, he knows his life could be so much more, but in order to get there he is going to have to do something he has never done and do it in a way he has never tried.

That something begins with him simply choosing to stick up for himself and not be so nice for a change. To a nice guy that sounds about as simple with jumping over the Grand Canyon on a two-wheeled tricycle, but it really is the starting point. When he has had enough of wearing the mask 24/7, is ready to tell the truth, and is honestly ready to step into his power as a man, that is when he will start.

If this is you, it is critically important for you to realize that this does not mean you become a jerk. It does not mean you minimize or mistreat others, it does not mean you are to act cruel, or that you intentionally hurt people.

What this does mean is that you choose to put you first for a change. And that idea alone (putting yourself first), if you are stuck in this trap as a nice guy, will already make your heart rate increase and make your breathing pattern change.

When you live life as a nice guy you are living life half–way. When you're wearing the mask of the nice guy, you are never who you were meant to be: not to yourself, not to your wife, not to your children, and not to God.

As the nice guy, you become trapped in the approval of others, trapped in the acceptance of others, trapped in the need for validation to come from everyone else—and you act accordingly. You become stuck seeking someone else to give you permission for what you are doing and what you want to do. If you don't get the pre–approval, then you don't even try.

In order for you to live life as a significant man, you have to break out of the mold of the nice guy, and it won't be easy.

If that's you, realize that you became the nice guy you are today over years of allowing the world to shape you that way. It may have started with seeking the constant approval of your mother, and that evolved into the seeking of constant approval from your wife—which is a clear sign of a man who is stuck as a nice guy.

In an ironic twist for nice guys, one of the common reasons for discontent between the nice guy and his wife is the fact that she says he is too nice! When he eventually decides to cross the line and decides that he is going to change, he can absolutely expect that there will be pushback, there will be arguments, and there will be stress, all while this change is taking place.

That, by itself, is what prevents most nice guys from ever going down this path. The nice guy hears that if he makes a change, if he chooses another path, there might be an argument, there might be stress, there might be pushback and his wife might not approve… so he will choose to stay where he is.

The nice guy is much happier to remain in the middle, without the tension, and never live a complete life, than he is willing to face the reality of what will happen when he decides to change. The nice guy will end up choosing a bland, boring, average, safe, and uneventful life.

Gentlemen, your wife wants you to lead, she wants you to step up, she wants you to do these things, and when you are stuck in nice guy mode, you cannot. Stop asking her what she wants for dinner, where she wants to go, what movie she wants to see, and so on… It is actually exhausting her that you ask her everything, all the time. She wants you to lift that exhaustion from her shoulders, so stop asking about every little thing!

Note: Please remember from the chapter, The Woman and The Nice Guy, nowhere do you have the ok to become an uncaring jerk.

Now go ahead, step up and plan dinner and a movie all on your own. Even if she ends up disliking your choice, she will be glad that you finally made a choice.

Yes, it might not go well. Yes, your decision might be the wrong one. Yes, you could fall flat on your face. You have to learn to accept that reality as you grow. If the evening doesn't go well, you learn from that, change your plan next time, and keep going. Do not allow yourself never to try again.

Until you are willing to risk coming in last, you will never come in first.

Thirty-Nine

WHAT IF YOU DON'T LIKE YOUR CALLING?

OK guys this is something I have been mulling about writing for a while, and decided it should be added to the book. I wrote this to perhaps make you think about a few things differently; you'll see plenty of questions in this chapter.

As a mentor, part of my work is to help men identify their true purpose and calling. Once identified, I work with these men to and build significant lives that take advantage of their purpose and calling.

It isn't always easy to find that purpose and that calling. Sometimes we go through times in life where our calling is elusive, or we identify our calling and we don't like it. What then?

What do we do if we don't like our calling? Or even worse, what if our calling seems, at least to us, to be utterly useless and insignificant?

Or how about this, you feel like you are supposed to know your calling now, or you are supposed to get started with changing the world now. You feel like you shouldn't have to wait, you should just get on with it.

You feel that it is unfair to have to wait; you're supposed to start now. So let me ask you this question…

What did Jesus do for the first 30 years of his life?

I mean really, what did he do from his birth up until he was around 30? He sure wasn't changing the world yet, that's pretty obvious.

He was performing manual labor, working with rock and wood. Yes, he was a simple and common carpenter, one of many. His work was not glamorous, he was not leading a movement, he was not speaking to thousands, and he was not changing the world, he was simply working. Too often people forget that Jesus was a working man, before he was changing the world.

He likely just went to do his work, probably complained about it from time to time, and then went home for the night. His hands probably got plenty of cuts and splinters. His sweat probably stung in his eyes. His body probably ached after yet another day, week, month, and year of this manual labor.

What do you think Jesus did during those years? Do you think he sent a text message to his friends complaining that he was not fulfilling his calling? Do you think he got online and posted a status update about how hard his life was? Did he write a blog about how he was not where he knew he was supposed to be, by this point of his life?

Maybe he had a video chat with some people, told them all how unfair his life was, and how it seemed like everything was against him. Maybe he was playing some video games with friends, and he was talking about how he didn't want to go into work another day.

While we're thinking about this, let's go a level deeper.

Where was God during the first three decades in the life of Jesus? Why didn't God simply deliver Jesus into a life where Jesus would live as a King from the moment he was born?

Was God somehow displeased with Jesus? Had Jesus done something wrong so that God was punishing him with this seemingly insignificant work and manual labor?

Did Jesus himself feel like he was insignificant during this time?

We are all going to have times where what we do feels insignificant, and where we do not like what we are called to do at those times, and from our own perspective.

Not every day and every year is going to be perfect. Not every job or every project is going to be fun. Even if you create your own business and are in control of your life, not everything is going to go as planned every day.

But, so what? What is your choice? To stop working, to stop engaging with life, to stop being with other people, to stop living? To stop providing for those who count on you? That is no choice at all.

The need for significance is strong in many people, but it is often much stronger in men than women. As men, we have a hard–wired need to do something significant with the work we do in our lives. This need can make us miss the opportunities right in front of us, on a daily basis.

We need to learn to find the significance in the everyday aspects of our lives, to find the opportunity that we have today, right now.

Because it might very well be that the work you are doing, at this moment, is work you don't like. It might very well be that the work you are doing today actually makes you feel insignificant, creating a void you feel inside.

So fill that void elsewhere. Help someone. Donate. Volunteer. Smile. Love!

It might also very well be that the calling you have in your life, right now, isn't one that you are aware of, isn't at your job, and if you aren't looking up—you might miss it.

A little while back, I was at the gas station. There was a couple, with a child in the back seat of their old, beat up, dirty car, and they were arguing. I could tell that they were not really arguing at each other, but just at life and in frustration. I overheard that they just made it to the gas station before they had to push the car, but they had no money to put gas in the tank.

Now I know, from painful personal experience, what it is like to fill the gas tank using a handful of change instead of a wallet full of paper or plastic. That is a sinking feeling, something that hits you deep in the gut, and something you do not ever want to have happen, especially as a man trying to provide for your family.

I waited a moment, until they were quiet, and walked over to them.

I mentioned that I overheard their conversation, and wanted to help them out. I made it very clear I wanted nothing in return. The man proudly shook his head, and I understood why.

So I looked at him and said, "Sir, I have been exactly where you are. All I would ask is that you please allow me to do this, and in the future you repay this same gesture when you find someone you can do this for."

He reluctantly said yes, and so I filled up their car with gas, to the top. It was probably the first time they had a full tank of gas in a long time. I said thank you to the husband, and then I walked over to his wife, gave her a $20 bill, so she could go inside and get something for her family.

I could see the tears in her eyes, and I could see the gratitude in his eyes. I shook both their hands, waved to the child in the back seat, got in my car and left.

To be honest, this was not something I did when I had tons of money overflowing in my own bank account. I most certainly could have used the money for my own family and our own needs. However, at that moment it was clearly the right thing to do for them.

For all I know, that one moment was my true calling, that single moment may have been my reason for being here on Earth. Yes, I work with lots of men, and I know that I have had a positive result on lots of families, but I do not truly know which one, where, when, why, how, etc... the real calling is coming from.

That husband could have been on the very edge of his life, and my gesture to him was the difference between him being here and not being here the next day. He may have been considering that one decision that would change everything.

You could be doing the very same thing. If your finances are tight right now, it doesn't need to be monetary help. Holding the door open, smiling at a stranger, offering to help someone carry something heavy, listening to a friend who needs someone to talk with.... none of that costs one penny.

We often misplace our calling and significance to where WE want it to be, right now—but that is not how life works, and that sure isn't how God works.

What you are doing and experiencing right now might simply be training for your future calling. The challenges and setbacks you are working through today might be so that you can teach and lead others through similar times in the future. The obstacles you have already overcome may have been there in your life so that you could become an example or mentor for others.

From my experience, those years of struggle and challenge were not years where I was living my calling, but they were some of the best years of preparation I could ever ask for. While I would not want anyone to go through what I went through, I also am grateful that I did. I learned more during those years, where I clearly was not living my calling, than I could ever describe.

My entire work with Significant Man wouldn't even exist had I not gone through the trials and painful times of my own past. Now I know that those times were training, they were education, they were there for me to learn entirely new things and become an even more effective mentor.

Our real calling, our real significance, it comes from how we lead our lives. It comes from the people we influence. It comes from the relationships we build. It comes from the legacy we create. And, it comes from how we leave the world once we are gone.

Forty
MAN, MONEY, AND GOD

*I*n my primary work, and at the live events I lead, the men I mentor are often entrepreneurs, business owners, or men who have control over their own financial destiny and decisions. The topic of money comes up often, as it should in that context.

Something that lots of men struggle with is the concept of making money, as it relates to being a Christian man. There is a misconception that to be a Christian you must not have wealth or that you must not become rich.

One reason that men feel this way is that so many people they see, who do have much and who are very rich, do not live a Christian life. It is not hard for any of us to see this.

We see the greed, we see the gluttony, we see the excess, all in people who are wealthy and not living in a manner we would. In turn, this leads many to associate those things with having money. Even if we didn't mean to, we end up equating money with being a bad person, someone we would never want to be, someone we would never want to emulate, etc…

What happens then is that we end up subconsciously stopping ourselves from reaching our goals. We don't go after the opportunity, because if we do—

we *might* end up rich. And, we "just know" that rich people are jerks, they are greedy, they are the reason for the bad in the world, and so on.

Look at how our society currently views people who have earned great wealth. They are derided, they are insulted, and they are viewed as abusers, as people who have only gotten where they are through taking advantage of others, and so on. That leads to a natural mindset and thought of "I don't want to be one of those people", which creates internal limitations and which stops many people from working towards their income goals.

However, you have to get rid of that mindset. If you want to have financial success, you have to lose those thoughts, and I mean you have to work to lose them right now.

Are there bad and greedy people, who happen to have lots of money? Of course. There are plenty of people who worship money, who use it as a weapon, who hold it over the head of others, who flaunt it, and so on, those people are simply part of life. Those people have been around in all cultures and all societies through the ages.

There are also bad and greedy people, who have little money. They steal and take what they can, without regard for anyone else other than themselves. Those people have also been around in all cultures and all societies throughout the ages.

On the flipside, there are plenty of wonderful people who are very wealthy, and who are kind, generous, giving, and loving. I know a gentleman who is worth nine figures (for real, not just on paper); he is the kind of man who could walk into almost any room and be on the highest financial rung of the ladder, the kind of man who could buy a business on a whim (but is smart enough not to).

You would never know his net worth by meeting him. He is happy to eat at a regular family restaurant. He is not demanding of the staff, he is kind and thanks them for their service—and then leaves them a generous tip after the meal.

What you have to learn is that money does not define you. Money does not turn you from a kind and loving person into a greedy person. Money also does not turn you from a greedy and mean person in a giving and caring person.

If you are kind and loving before you are wealthy, you still will be after you are wealthy. If you are greedy and mean before you are wealthy, you still will be after you are wealthy. Money is simply an amplifier.

The reality of this world is that you need money, you need it for your family, and you need it to change the world. If you want to run a business, you need money. If you want to change your community, you need money, and if you want to help people, you need money.

How many people can you help if you do not have anything to give them? (Excluding your time and love, of course). How many meals can you buy for the homeless? How many warm coats can you provide? How much can you affect your church? How much can you give to a shelter?

How much water can you pour out of an empty glass?

God and Jesus both had plenty to say about money. Nowhere does the Bible state that money is evil. I'm sure you have heard the phrase, "Money is the root of all evil." as one based in the Bible. Many of you might know, and for others this will be a revelation, that phrase is *not* a biblical phrase.

The biblical phrase specifically is, "For the *love of money* is a root of all kinds of evil." There is a world of difference between those phrases. Loving the money means that you have turned money into a false idol, and that you have lost the truth that money is just a resource to use.

In other words, it is loving money that is the problem, not money itself nor even earning lots of money. The problem is when the focus of your love is the actual money.

In the five talents parable, you can see that God actually wants you to be successful, He wants you to use what He has given you, He wants you to multiply what you have been given. So yes, God wants you to have success.

If you don't know the five talents parable and you want to go check it out, you can find it in Matthew 25: 14–30 (I'll include it below for reference).

God wants you to know that your success is a result of your work, do the work. God wants you to know that He has given you what you need in order to succeed, use what He gave you.

And perhaps most importantly, and something that can make us uneasy when we accept this truth, God wants you to know that you will be held accountable for what you do with your talents. If you don't use what you have been given, that is not a good thing!

Men, you need to understand this. It is critical. God wants you to have success, and there is nothing wrong with doing so.

When you get this your business can change, your outlook can change, and your future can change. It really is one of those big life-changing concepts to grasp, and it might take a while to get there—but when you get there, you are now seeing life with a brand new perspective.

Now go get out there, and start using the talents He gave you!

Lastly, about the following passages: the reason that this is called the parable of the Five Talents, and not the parable of gold is due to the original Greek. The Greek use of "talent" was a unit of measurement; a talent was worth about 20 years of a laborer's wages. Modern versions, such as the NIV, have replaced talent with gold, to be clearer to the modern reader.

Matthew 25:14–30 New International Version (NIV)

The Parable of the Five Talents

"Again, it will be like a man going on a journey, who called his servants and entrusted his wealth to them. To one he gave five bags of gold, to another two bags, and to another one bag, each according to his ability. Then he went on his journey. The man who had received five bags of gold went at once and put his money to work and gained five bags more. So also, the one with two bags of gold gained two more. But the man who had received one bag went off, dug a hole in the ground and hid his master's money.

"After a long time the master of those servants returned and settled accounts with them. The man who had received five bags of gold brought the other five. 'Master,' he said, 'you entrusted me with five bags of gold. See, I have gained five more.'

"His master replied, 'Well done, good and faithful servant! You have been faithful with a few things; I will put you in charge of many things. Come and share your master's happiness!'

"The man with two bags of gold also came. 'Master,' he said, 'you entrusted me with two bags of gold; see, I have gained two more.'

"His master replied, 'Well done, good and faithful servant! You have been faithful with a few things; I will put you in charge of many things. Come and share your master's happiness!'

"Then the man who had received one bag of gold came. 'Master,' he said, 'I knew that you are a hard man, harvesting where you have not sown and gathering where you have not scattered seed. So I was afraid and went out and hid your gold in the ground. See, here is what belongs to you.'

"His master replied, 'You wicked, lazy servant! So you knew that I harvest where I have not sown and gather where I have not scattered seed? Well then, you should have put my money on deposit with the bankers, so that when I returned I would have received it back with interest.

"So take the bag of gold from him and give it to the one who has ten bags. For whoever has will be given more, and they will have an abundance. Whoever does not have, even what they have will be taken from them. And throw that worthless servant outside, into the darkness, where there will be weeping and gnashing of teeth."

Forty-One
YOU ARE NOT YOUR CAREER

One major problem for men, especially in Western society, is the association and confusion we make between value, worth, identity, and our careers. As a result, we often end up looking to our careers to prove our value, to give us an identity, and to define our worth. We end up associating our career with who we are, so closely and in such a tight manner, that our career ends up actually defining us as men.

That association is extraordinarily dangerous.

Where and how did this start? What do we do about it? Before we can get into what to do about this, we have to know the origins, and to do that we have to go deep on the sorts of questions I love asking.

Let me ask you this, what does it mean to be a man? How do you define a man?

If you're like most men, in your response to those questions your career and finances will be immediate answers. That includes a primary driving force of being able to provide for your family and for those you love. Additionally, since the provider answer is in there, the source of income for that provision is part of the equation. We look at our careers as where the providing comes from.

What happens is that we associate our own value, in this case the money we earn and provide, with our careers and therefore with who we each are as a man. If we don't earn enough money, if we aren't providing, we mentally torture ourselves, questioning our very worth and value to our family and society.

If we don't provide enough, the internal pain and internal conversations we have, about our purpose and value to those we love, become the focus of our thoughts, every minute of every day. Our worth, as men, ends up directly tied to our income. Which then leads to our careers becoming who we are, and again that is extraordinarily dangerous.

To make this more complex, there is the pursuit of making the career itself a source of satisfaction and fulfillment. While having a career that is positive and satisfying definitely isn't a negative thing to pursue (it's actually wonderful!), the pursuit can lead to confusion and pain.

It is great to have a career that does provide everything you want; I truly love my work and helping men become more. I love hearing from wives about the changes their husbands made. I love hearing from men who are now empowered to live life. However, the pursuit of such a career can become the pursuit of a goal that is going to remain just out of reach, no matter how much money you earn.

If you spend your life trying to reach for something that is always just a few inches away, that something soon becomes a source of disillusionment and unhappiness.

If your career as a source of great happiness and satisfaction is an unmet goal, that weighs on your mind even more. You see other men who seem to have careers they love, and might ask yourself, why can't I have that? You see other men who get great joy from their work, and you might think, that is how I should live, and until I do, I can't be happy.

When that happens, we have transferred our ability to experience happiness and satisfaction to our career. We have given away our own power to define those critical areas of life to our career, and that, as well, is extraordinarily dangerous.

So, what do we do, what is the solution here?

What we have to do, absolutely have to do, is to disassociate who we are, as men, with our careers. There is massive pushback on this, in our society. Anytime

I talk about this, I hear the pushback, including the pushback in my own mind to be honest, but that will not change this point.

I like, and use, this great quote, from Martin Luther King, Jr. He said, "What I'm saying to you this morning, my friends, even if it falls your lot to be a street sweeper, go on out and sweep streets like Michelangelo painted pictures; sweep streets like Handel and Beethoven composed music; sweep streets like Shakespeare wrote poetry; sweep streets so well that all the host of heaven and earth will have to pause and say, "Here lived a great street sweeper who swept his job well."

As men, we take that quote to mean that we should do our jobs the best we can. That is true; we should be doing our jobs to the best of our ability. As a man, you better be working as hard and as effectively as you can. However, there is so much more to this concept, it goes so much deeper.

You see, it isn't just about doing our jobs well. We had all better do that, that should be a given, we should be expected to do our work well. Will we have some days that aren't so great? Of course, but on the whole we should always be striving to do our best, every single day.

Beyond that, we need to learn that no matter what our job is, that job is not what gives us our identity. The man who is a street sweeper who sweeps like Beethoven will never be known as a street sweeper. While the street sweeper who just works hard every day will be known as a street sweeper.

The man who learns that his job is not who he is, is like the street sweeper who has learned to sweep streets like Shakespeare wrote poetry. No one will know him as simply a street sweeper; he will be known as an artist, as a man who is living on the next level.

Sometimes this sort of topic also requires a more global perspective, leaving Western society.

Let me ask you this. How is it possible that a man in a third world country could follow elephants all day long for years, and is the person responsible for cleaning up the elephant dung on the streets, yet he does not question his own identity?

How is that possible? How can that man not be lost in the questions about purpose, motivation, and identity as a man?

Because he has learned that his career is not who he is, as a man. He has learned that behind that work, behind his career, are people who are reaping the benefits and rewards of what he is doing. He has learned that those reasons are powerful and are why he does what he does. He is not doing that work because the work itself defines him, he is doing it because he knows that he will go home, after a long hard day of work, and put food on the table for his family. He knows he is providing for his family. He knows that he is a man leading those he loves and cares for.

Bringing it back here then, to a more Western view on this subject.

As mentioned earlier in this chapter, for most men our career often becomes our identity. This is one of the cornerstones of the old question, when first meeting another man, "So, what do you do?"

As discussed in the first chapter, men use this question to establish a pecking order, to see who makes the most money, who sits highest on the success ladder, who has the most prestige, and so on… in other words, the career we have becomes intrinsically tied into who we are.

What happens then if we find ourselves disliking our career? If our career is part of our identity, that means that somewhere inside us, we now have some dislike towards ourselves.

What happens then if we find a career change forced onto us, such as losing our job or if the company closes? When our career is our identity that means we have just had a piece of ourselves lost or closed.

What happens then if we find that our career is no longer satisfying? If our career is part of our identity, that means that we begin to question our own lives having satisfaction.

What happens then if we find our career seems to have no bigger purpose? If our career is part of our identity, that means we subconsciously think we have no purpose. We feel reduced to nothing other than a paycheck generator.

Disliking ourselves, having a piece of ourselves removed, living without satisfaction, and feeling reduced to nothing, all from creating this association between career and identity.

OK, so what is the solution? Well, it is easy and it is hard, all at the same time. It is easy for me to tell you, and hard to put that into practice over time.

Here is the short answer: Disassociate your career from your identity and worth as a man. Period.

Does your career matter? Of course. Should you try to have a career that provides you more than just money? Of course. Should you be actively trying to create and build the opportunity for that to happen? Of course. However, let's go with the worst-case scenario: meaning you will never have a career you love, and you will never create your own career opportunities. What then? How are you supposed to enjoy life?

That is where the disassociation comes into play. You need to do three things:

First, sweep the streets as if you are Beethoven composing music. Sweep them at such a level that no one in their right mind, will actually think of you as a street sweeper. Have people look at your work and results with awe and wonder, no matter what that work is. In other words, what you do to earn an income, is nothing compared to who you are and the level at which you do that work.

Second, learn to focus on the result of what the work provides for you. Take pride in your work, yes, but do not lose sight of the big picture results that your work has provided. Your work is what allows you to live in a culture that has air conditioning, restaurants, hot water, electricity, and so on…

That is not a trivial point, and too often guys will read past something like that, without really spending time to digest the impact there. Directly because of your work today, you and your family get to enjoy comforts and opportunities that most of human history never even dreamed of.

Even if you are not yet where you want to go, in terms of the kinds of comforts and opportunities you will provide for your family, you still are enjoying what was beyond the reach of Kings in the past. Never lose that perspective.

Third, and perhaps most importantly, get back in touch with your powerful *why* as a man. As a man, what is your true purpose here on Earth, why are you here? You are not here to have a specific career, or to earn a specific income. You are here to love, to protect, to lead, to grow, to share, to set an example, to mentor, to teach, to experience, to overcome, to build, to create, to take risks, to inspire, to be bold, to question, to answer, to be a gentleman, to serve others, to provide, and to love (yes love is worth two mentions).

Not one of those things requires you to have any specific career or to have any specific income level. You can do every single one of them, regardless of where your income comes from or how much you currently earn.

You are not your career, whether you do or don't have your dream career. You are not your career. Careers can, and will, always change. So do not allow your inner voice, or our society, to say that you are your career.

Instead, rise up and show the world that you will sweep the streets like Michelangelo painted paintings, and that you will become a significant man.

Forty-Two

LET THEM FALL

*I*t sure can be confusing for men becoming fathers today. Especially with children in their younger years, from birth through about 7 years old, there aren't many excellent resources for men trying to be great fathers. There are some entertaining blogs, which tend towards simple and fun things like doing braids for daughters, cooking, and other safe topics.

But about the big and important stuff? There simply isn't much out there for men who are seeking to be the best fathers they can be. So men tend to fall back into the things that come naturally, they will play sports and other fun activities with their kids, and they will make silly voices, sing silly songs, tell silly jokes, and all the other great things us dads get to do.

Too often however, that is where it ends with men. The easy stuff. The simple stuff.

That stuff is really important, please don't misunderstand. The time you spend playing with your kids, being silly with them, laughing and loving, that is all critically important to them, and to you. Your children need to know that you are that kind of dad for them.

But there is more. There is more work for you to do as a father, work that isn't easy like playing, laughing, and having fun is. You have to teach your kids through the more challenging parts of growing up.

It is becoming harder to do some of these important things in our society. Today it seems like the goal is to protect children, at all costs, and to make sure that there is constant vigilance towards ensuring that children don't experience discomfort, pain, or any other challenging situations.

Choosing that goal is a major mistake. You want your kids to experience those hard things.

You want to let your kids fall.

As fathers, this is not easy. We have a built-in drive to protect. We will protect our family at all costs; it is part of who we are. We see risky situations and mitigate them before anything bad even happens. However, in this case I'm talking about something a bit different.

I'm talking about you training and raising your kids into adults. I'm talking about you doing your part to ensure that your kids become good men and women themselves, ready to contribute and grow into more than you could ever imagine.

This job, training and raising your kids, is unique for a father. There is nothing else like it, anywhere in your life. This is part of your legacy, part of how you will leave the world a better place when you are gone.

This is where you change generations. You are going to pass things onto the next generation, that will absolutely happen, and this is where you decide what those things are going to be.

Too often today, parents jump in to save their children from anything that might be hard or challenging. Parents will do their children's homework, ensuring the child gets good grades. If the child isn't getting a good enough grade, then the parent heads to the school to make the teacher change the grade. That's insane!

Parents end up removing all situations that could require their child to learn how to cope with disappointment, deal with problems, or overcome obstacles.

These parents are trying well and they mean well, but as the old saying states, the path to hell is paved with good intentions. It doesn't matter if you mean well, doing this to your child is harmful. Doing this to your sons and daughters means they will lack the skills to navigate the world, they will become much more dependent on others (you, friends, family, and/or the government), and they will have a hard time considering new ideas and options in their own lives.

So let them fall. Maybe even fall hard sometimes.

One place I frequently saw the overprotective dads was on the playground. As a father of four, there were plenty of trips to the playground. I could write an entire parenting book just on experiences at the playground!

While I was there with them (because it seems to be a crime in parts of this country to let your kids go to the playground on their own these days) I could (usually) see where they were, and I didn't stand right over them.

Far too many parents are right next to their child, every step of the way. Fathers holding their kids up on the playground equipment, being at the bottom of the slide, walking them over to the ladder to head back up, every second they were only inches away. Fathers ensuring that, no matter what their child did, there would never be any failure or challenge.

I remember a time when one of my daughters fell pretty hard, and she was on the ground crying. I could see her; I saw exactly what happened. I knew she had no physical injury, and could see that her tears were a combination of hurt pride and anger at falling.

A random mom rushed over to her and started coddling her. From where I was sitting, I said, "She's fine, let her get up please." The mom looked at me with obvious disgust; clearly, she thought I was the worst father in the world. Thankfully, she walked away.

My daughter sat there for a moment, and after realizing I wasn't coming to pick her up, she picked herself up. The very next minute she was back up and trying again, and this time she didn't fall. She was beaming with pride at what she had accomplished on her own.

We need to learn to trust our children more, including trusting them to handle pain and failure. Yes, we absolutely have to be there to protect our children and to help them. And yes, it is very hard to see your child hurting, no parent ever likes that. But children are far more amazing and powerful than most parents give them credit for.

Part of your job, as a father, is to prepare your children to overcome obstacles, to learn that they can do things they might not think they can do, and to experience what it feels like to fail at something, only to come back and succeed the next time.

Your children are incredible. They can do incredible things. They can become wonderful adults.

Especially if you let them fall.

Forty-Three
REMEMBER YOUR QUEEN

To start here, we're going to take a trip down memory lane…

Remember.

Remember when you first saw her? There she was, suddenly in your view and the rest of the world faded away. Time slowed down and the music stopped playing. You knew right then. You knew she was the one.

You noticed everything about her. You noticed her eyes, her hair, her lips, her curves, her body, her smile, her smell, her skin; she was intoxicating, you never had noticed anyone that way before. She was the most beautiful woman you had ever seen. She took your breath away. When you were going to have a date with her, your entire day was better; it didn't matter what happened during the day because you knew that you would see her that night.

Remember.

Remember when you talked with her for hours? Remember when you laughed and shared and loved? Remember how she made you feel? It was like you were the King of the world, and that nothing could stop you.

She was your Queen. Together the two of you were going to do amazing things. Together you were partners who would change the world. Together you had hopes, dreams, and ambitions.

Slowly, likely without even realizing it, life showed up and made you weary. The constant pressure of work, of earning an income, of raising the children, of cleaning the house, of meeting obligations and responsibilities, and you ended up quietly eating lukewarm leftovers for dinner on Saturday night. The nights of fun and hopeful expectation about the future dissolved into slipping into a cold bed early, hoping to sleep well enough to make it through the day tomorrow.

This is the reality for more men that you may ever know. Over the years, I have heard man after man after man tell me a similar story, always with great sadness in his voice. This is not what he had in mind for his marriage, and this is not was he was expecting his future to be like.

Yet, here he is. Perhaps this is where you are as well.

It is time to make another choice, and time to get to work. This will begin with you and is about the relationship you have with your queen.

She is still in there, the beautiful, powerful, and wonderful woman that you knew when you were first dating. She is still in there, the curious, helpful, and amazing woman that you first fell in love with.

She needs you to step up and become the king again. She needs you to wake up and become the man that she first fell in love with. She needs you to rise up and become the man that she knows you have inside, waiting to come back to life.

Remember.

Remember when you were dating? Remember the anticipation of the evening? Remember making the dinner plans, finding a new restaurant that you wanted to experience with her? Remember taking her home after dinner? Remember the first time you kissed her goodnight after a date? Remember the first time you felt the warmth of her skin?

When was the last time you took your queen out on a date? When was the last time you bought her flowers for no reason? When was the last time you called her, just to talk to her? When was the last time you texted her, during the middle of your busy day, something that will make her smile?

It is far too easy to let life get in the way of this, far too easy to say you are too tired or too busy to do those things, and if you do… you are making a major mistake.

It is far too easy to let chores and work get in the way, far too easy to say you have to work on the car, or repair the hot water heater than it is to spend time with your wife.

It is far too easy to think that you will recharge during an annual vacation. It is far too easy to think that you will reconnect in ten years when the kids have gone to college.

The relationship you have with her is the most important one in your life, more than with your kids, more than with your friends, it is her. She is your Queen, you have to invest in your relationship.

You need to choose to become that man again right now, or become that man for the first time if you have never done this before. Create time in your life that is just for her, with no distractions. Take her out on date nights again. Get a hotel room. Go for a long walk. Buy her flowers. All of it.

Never stop dating her. Never take her for granted. Never expect that life will simply continue without you putting in the effort to have the connection with her that you really want to have, because it won't. This connection won't magically come back, if you let it die. You have to take action; you have to do the work.

It is time for you to "re–learn" how to date your wife, if that is what's required. It might be awkward at first, if you have let this slide too far, but is something you have to do. Just as you had to learn how to date her the first time, you may need to learn how to do this again. Yes, you might screw it up… but, so what? You're on a journey towards becoming a more significant man and this is part of that journey.

Have fun with it! Remember and think about how you wooed her, how you pursued her, how you loved every minute with her. Remember how you kept at it, you kept going, even if you messed up, because you knew she was the one. You just knew it in your soul.

She is right there, right now, waiting for you to do this. Maybe she is even sitting next to you, as you're reading this chapter.

Remember.

Now if this has been a while, here is a simple game plan for you to follow:

Step One: Call or text your wife, as soon as you're done reading this chapter, and tell her that you are taking her out tonight. Let her know that you are going to take care of everything.

Step Two: Call and make the reservations for dinner. Find a babysitter, if needed. Cancel any other plans that you had for tonight. Program the DVR if there was a show you wanted to watch.

Step Three: Tell her what time you have to leave, and what kind of restaurant you're going to. (This is so she knows how to dress and gives her enough time, don't skip this.)

Step Four: Leave the house and drive around the block. Come to the door and ring the doorbell. Escort her to the car. Open the door for her. (Bonus points if you go get a flower to give her at the door.)

Step Five: Take her to dinner, enjoy a nice slow meal, and give her your undivided attention. Make sure your put your mobile phone away.

That's it, that's enough. Start there. Then keep doing this and variations on this, until dating your queen becomes a regular part of your life again.

She deserves for you to treat her as your Queen, because she is your Queen!

Forty-Four
LIVE TOGETHER OR DIE ALONE

I don't watch much TV to be honest. I often find it a waste of time (though I watch lots of movies in my awesome home theater; I'm a major movie fan. And I acknowledge many find that to be a waste of time as well). There is one show I regularly watch with one of my incredible daughters and one show I watch with my amazing wife, but that's pretty much the limit of my regular TV watching.

However, I did watch and appreciate LOST when that show was on. It had some depth to it, lots of interesting characters and fascinating story lines, although it did get weird and had a bizarre disappointing ending. I liked watching that series with my family.

During one of the important scenes in the first season of the show, Jack, who eventually becomes the leader, had a great line:

"If we can't learn to live together, then we're going to die alone."

That is a powerful truth about so many aspects of our lives. That truth applies to important relationships you have all over your life.

It is obviously true for you and your wife. It's true for you and your kids. It's true for you and your friends. It's true for you and your mentors. It's true for you and those you mentor.

In other words, everywhere in your life, that is truth for your relationships. Either you learn to live together, or you die alone.

Living together isn't always easy, and when things get hard we look for a way out of the situation. Men have their ways of getting out of situations they don't want to be in.

The main ways out are to retreat into our fortress (where we think we can't get hurt), to hide behind our masks (where we think no one will see the real us), or to only engage with those who we already share everything in common (where we think we won't have our ideas and beliefs challenged).

When we have a challenge or conflict with someone, it is common then to pull back to easier times, to better times, and to when we could stay in our comfort zones. After all, no one really wants conflict, and no one really wants to be in those situations.

But in order to really live, to really embrace the life you have been given, you have to be willing to get out of your comfort zone. You have to be willing to experience the challenges of life and to challenge others in the same.

However, too often when the challenges come, most men will either choose to retreat into the safety of their fortress or to move on to somewhere else where they think they will find happiness. They will pick one of these two because they have decided it isn't worth the effort or the risk, and so they won't challenge themselves to become that significant man. Instead of growing into more, they will shrink backwards into smaller lives.

The first option, to retreat into the fortress is the most common option that men will take. This is the option where the man pulls back, he no longer talks about what is going on, he no longer engages in the challenge, the conflict, or the conversation. He thinks that if he simply pulls back into the safety of his fortress he will be able to ride out the storm.

And he is right, to a degree. He will be able to ride out the storm that is happening now, while inside his fortress. However, eventually he will have to come out into the wilderness where the challenges are, or he will die inside because he has nothing left to give him any energy. The inside of his fortress becomes a cold, dark, and uninviting place—a place with no challenges, and also no adventure, no battle, and no life.

The other option is taking place too often as well, and that's moving on to someplace new. This man has a fight with his wife, and instead of resolving the issue with her, he goes to seek another woman. This man has a challenge with his wife, blames her and tells her that he should have married someone else. This man places all the problems of his life on the shoulders of his wife, and then he storms out of the house.

This man has an argument with his children, and becomes a disengaged father. This man has a problem with his business, and so he gives up on his dreams. This man finds comfort, solace, and understanding from another woman, and so he moves on.

Both of those options cause pain and isolation. Retreating back into the fortress might give the man a temporary peace from his challenge, but it will ultimately create an unhappy life of living alone, with no one else allowed inside. Moving on, hoping to find happiness in the arms of another leaves his family broken, his children in pain, and his wife with confusion and unanswered guilt.

Both of those solutions are very likely to end up creating a generations–long effect. The children who see this behavior learn that this is how a man, a husband, a father, is supposed to act. Sons grow up to repeat what the father did, and daughters grow up to marry a man like the father. The cycle continues for another generation.

There are so many stories like this, of men retreating and of men moving on. I've heard them. You've heard them. They are unfortunately all around us, not hard to find. That sort of man seems to be everywhere, and that sort of man is not yet on his way to becoming a significant man.

You can choose differently. You can choose to walk on neither of those paths. You can choose to not retreat into your fortress and you can choose not to move on. You can go through the challenge, go through the conflict, and have the difficult conversations.

You can become the father you want to be, a man who is fully present with your children, leading them through difficult times, and not leaving those conversations up to your wife. You can raise up and teach your children.

You can become the husband you want to be, enjoying a powerful and intimate connection with your wife, becoming a man who is willing to have the hard conversations together, coming out a stronger partnership on the other side.

You can become the man that others can turn to and can count on. You have to become the man that can hear the burdens of your brothers.

You can become the man that can be the trusted rock for someone else.

You have to be willing to walk through the challenge, walk through the conflict and learn to grow together. We all have to be willing to experience the pain, learn from it, and become more together.

In other words, you have to learn to live together, so that you don't die alone.

Forty-Five
YOU WERE CALLED TO LEAD

In my live events, when I'm working with men and we are walking through their lives and their families, and then get to their careers, there is a common issue that comes up. You see many of the men I work with have an unmet desire, a deep longing in their souls for something more they want to achieve in their work.

They know they have more to offer, they know they were created for more on this Earth, they are 100% sure of this, but there is just one problem. I'm going to use Joe again here in the discussion, but this is a similar conversation and question to one I've had with lots of different men, over the years. Perhaps this sounds familiar to what you have thought yourself:

Joe and I are working through the process together and Joe is clearly a man who is seeking the most out of life and who wants to do the right things. Joe is one of those men who has had enough, and who wants to choose a new life, to become the man that he knows he can be.

Joe is trying hard; he is a good man. Joe has faith, he has desire, he is a driven man, he is smart, and he knows that he there is much more he can do.

Joe tells me what so many others have shared; that he feels he has a calling higher than just making money, that he has a higher purpose than just having fun, and that he was created for more.

There is one problem, and it's a major problem in Joe's mind.

Joe has had problems at home. He and his wife are not always on the greatest terms. He and his kids are not on the same page as he thinks they should be. He and God don't connect in a deep and meaningful way. He has stepped up and owned his situation, and this leads to the problem.

Joe isn't on the edge anymore, even though he used to be. Joe isn't thinking of any drastic decision, he isn't going to separate from his wife, he isn't screaming at his kids... there is none of that. However, things aren't all great, there are problems in his life. He wants to grow and become a mentor and a leader, but the problem keeps coming back to him.

Joe describes the problem when he tells me that he keeps thinking, "How can I lead other men, how can I be an example, how can I be a mentor, when I can't even take care of everything in my own house? How can I lead others, when I have my own problems? Who am I to have those thoughts in the first place? I know that I'm meant for more, but feel like a fraud here."

And there it is. The feeling of being a fraud. The feeling that is often at the heart and soul of the pain that is inside so many men.

Have you felt the same thing? Have you felt called to do more, knowing in your gut that you have so much more to offer the world, but at the same time you hold yourself back because you feel like your own house isn't 100% in perfect order and you don't currently enjoy the mythical "I have it all" status in your mind?

I know that exact feeling. I have felt those exact thoughts. When I first heard the call to lead other men, my life was not where I wanted it to be. I had lots of work to do in my relationship with my wife. I had lots of work to do in leading my children. I had lots of work to do in connecting with God. I had screwed up plenty, I had made lots of mistakes, and I knew there was lots I had to learn (and I'm still learning more every single day).

So I know that feeling. I know those thoughts. I've been there, and I can tell you this:

You can start leading today, right now. You can start becoming that significant man today, right now. This is a lifelong journey you are on, if you decide to really live this way and go down this road, you will still be learning and growing while on your deathbed.

You can't wait to get started, there is too much at stake. You can start making new choices today, right now. Even the moment you finish reading this chapter, that is a perfect time to make new choices and to get started.

You can start leading your children. You can show them that you are willing to stand up and do the right thing. You can show your children how to become better themselves. You can teach them with your actions. You can teach them with your words. You can teach them with the games you play and the conversations you share. You can start that today, right now.

You can have the conversation with your wife that you have been putting off. You can take off the mask and share the real you with her. You can begin to build that bridge. You can start taking small steps to become the husband you know you can be. You can start that today, right now.

As a leader, doing what you were called to do is leading.

No one—NO ONE—has it all and has everything figured out, despite what they might say in their marketing and when they are boasting. The men you see leading other organizations have their own problems and challenges, they are simply different from your problems and challenges. Don't believe the lie for one minute that there is some magic formula to having a perfect life where everything just falls into your lap and problems disappear.

What you don't want to do, and where men often get stuck on this, is trying to lead someone else to a place that they have never gone themselves. If you have never climbed to the top of a mountain, then no, you shouldn't be trying to lead others in mountain climbing. If you have never built a business, then you shouldn't be trying to lead others in building their own business.

However, you can still lead. You can still help others, be a mentor, and show the ropes to those who are seeking what you have to offer.

Imagine you are climbing a mountain, and you are leading other men. Can you still lead, even if you are not the first person on the rope? Absolutely. You can lead the men who are behind you, the men who are not as experienced as you are.

When you get to a tough part of the climb, you can turn around and hold out your hand to pull the man behind you up. You can lead him to where you have already gone. This can happen while you are learning from the man in front of you.

We are all both leaders and followers, at the same time. We should all be mentors to others while we learn from our own mentors. We should always be both, all the time. We should be learning from the mentors, coaches, and teachers we have selected, and we should be leading others at the same time.

What you can do is start today, you can lead the men who are in your sphere of influence, you can start becoming a mentor, you can start becoming that leader you have inside. Don't try to lead them to places you've never gone, but you can go ahead and lead them through the challenges you have already gone through.

You don't need to keep waiting. You don't need to get another degree. You don't need to attend another webinar. You don't need any of that to get started. You can start leading others today.

As a leader, you do not need to pretend you have all the answers or that you never fall yourself. Everyone falls. You do. I do. Every single one of us falls, we're human.

As a leader, you are willing to step up and do what most won't do. That is what makes you a leader. It isn't that all of your life is perfectly in line.

As a leader, you are willing to embrace falling and failing because you know that is when you experience the most growth. It isn't that you will never fail.

As a leader, you are willing to keep learning, to keep growing, to keep investing, to keep doing what you have to do so that next year you will not be in the same situation you're in this year.

If you are called to lead, if you have heard that voice in the back of your mind telling you that you are here for more… it's time to get to work and lead.

Forty-Six

HIGHLIGHT REAL

*H*ave you ever wondered why using social media can often lead to feeling depressed and anxious, and noticed that it can lead to feelings of inadequacy and incompetence? In other words, not good feelings.

There actually is a simple reason for this.

The reason is that when you are online, when you are scrolling through social media and you are seeing all the great pictures, the amazing videos, and reading the wonderful stories, you are seeing the Highlight Reel you are not seeing the Real parts of life.

Meaning you are only seeing the best pictures, the best videos, the stories that show the person posting in the best light possible. In other words, you are seeing the highlight REEL.

You are not seeing the REAL.

And seeing that can be depressing. Imagine if every time you went to a social gathering, every single person you met showed up in a better car, wore better clothes, had an expensive watch, expensive shoes, had a beauty queen wife, had kids perfectly lined up in their perfectly matching outfits, all while using the latest new gadgets and technology. Then every single person talked about the incredible extended vacation that they took and the even more incredible vacation they have lined up next. And on and on it went.

(For this chapter I'm ignoring the fact that so many of those highlights are fake in the first place. I can tell you for a fact that many of those pictures of exotic sports cars are taken with one-hour rentals, those guys don't own those cars. And many of the homes aren't theirs either, they just park in front of them while driving around in their rented sports car.)

All that perfection, all those amazing homes, the amazing money, the amazing toys, the amazing cars, all those amazing stories, and all those amazing experiences shown right in front of you—it is too much for many to bear.

That leads directly to these thoughts in men:

- "I'll never have what he has."
- "I bet his wife respects him with all that."
- "I'll never succeed like him."
- "I don't even deserve success."
- "I'm a failure."
- "My family would be better off without me."

All because of what you see and read on social media. Imagine how you would feel if you were already questioning your ability and progress (and who hasn't?), and then you come online to see all the amazing things that other men have that you don't?

That thinking quickly and easily leads to seeing what he has which can lead to envy, which can lead to anger and depression. All from scrolling through social media.

It is important to recognize the initial trigger there is seeing the appearance of the other man's life. You see and read about what he has or has done and you compare that to your own reality.

You are comparing his Highlight Reel to your Real.

When you see and read about his success in life and start to think about your own life, those feelings start and those negative associations kick in. You start to think about all the things that haven't gone right in your life, you start to think about all the things that have gone right in his life. You might think how lucky he must be.

You see his cars. You see his homes. You see his income. You see his vacations, toys, and all the other things that the other man is showing in his Highlight Reel.

You look at your own real life, wonder where it went wrong, and wonder if it will ever go right. You wonder if you will ever be able to keep up with all the other cool kids. Suddenly it feels like High School all over again for many, wondering if this time around you'll get to sit at the cool kid's lunch table.

What you don't often realize is that the cool kids are falling completely apart when no one is looking. They are barely holding it together in their real lives, all while they pretend everything is perfect in their social media lives.

Here is the thing; here is where we turn this around.

You have to realize that you are not looking at their honest reality when you are on social media. You have to realize that you are looking at the equivalent of a TV show or movie, one that is scripted and with each shot taken with care to create the desired image.

By the way, some people literally have a photographer compose and take the pictures they post online. They script their lives to that level. Don't forget that.

The men with the perfect lives are not perfect, no matter what their Highlight Reel might look like. They get sick, they have bad days, they fight and argue with their wives and kids, they have messes in their homes, they have food under the seats of their cars, and they even go to the bathroom just like other humans!

The men who show their Highlight Reel have pain, they have hurt, they have sadness, they have guilt, they get depressed, and they are worried about how many people will Like their next post. Often these men have even greater guilt and depression, because they know they are living an image; they know, in their souls, that what they put out in public isn't real.

Your Real is far more important than someone else's Highlight Reel. The people in your life, the ones you love and the ones who love you, they are far more important than a posed picture in front of the Sphinx. The life you are living now, the experiences you have had and will have are far more important than a faked vacation photo from the International Space Station.

You have one life to live, and it is your Real Life. Be Real. Let the world see and know the Real You.

Forty-Seven

IT'S NOT ABOUT HER

When it comes to the woman in our lives, most men have major challenges. They try hard, no doubt. They try the best, no doubt. They try to be better husbands, no doubt.

Even with all that trying, there are challenges. There are challenges with communication, about what the future holds, about how to raise the kids, about finances, about church, about what TV show to watch, about what to eat, etc... The list of challenges sometimes seems endless, sometimes it seems like the list of things that aren't challenges would be smaller!

Because of these challenges, because of these conflicts, often I hear this sort of thing from the guys:

- "If she would just be less demanding, then things would be great."
- "If she would just have sex with me more, then things would be great."
- "If she would just stop controlling me, then things would be great."
- "If she would just stop asking me how I feel, then things would be great."
- "If she would just support me for a change, then things would be great."

- "If she would just let me be who I am, then things would be great."
- "If she would just stop telling me how to do everything, then things would be great."

On and on and on it goes…

As if all the challenges in the relationship are because of her, because of what she thinks, because of how she acts, and because of who she is. Now to be clear, is it true that she has to make changes herself? Yes. Does she have to make different choices as well? Yes. Does she need to learn more about you? Yes. Does she need to understand what you want out of life and your relationship? Of course, that is all absolutely true, but this book isn't to her it is to you. I'm not talking to her, I'm talking to you.

And to you, I have a very simple statement for you to realize:

It's Not About Her.

It is about you. It is about your choices. It is about your attitude. It is about what you are providing. It is about your leadership. It is about what you are willing to do and what you are not willing to do. It is about you.

Your job is to work on you, to stop lying to yourself about your situation, to take ownership of your reality, and to get busy doing what you know you need to do. Your job is to make new choices, take action on what you decide, and then to live your life as the significant man that God created you to be. You have the power and the responsibility to control all of that, no matter what she does.

Your wife most likely sees a man in you that you don't see yet. Women have the amazing ability to see who we can become way before us men ever do, and she is doing what she thinks is right and needed for you to become that man.

In other words, she wants you to become the significant man that you want to become. You both want the same thing; although the methods are very different so it doesn't always seem like you do want the same thing.

But you do.

Even though you want the same thing, the reality is that just as she is responsible for her, you are responsible for you. However, as mentioned earlier this chapter is to you, it's not about her. So let's talk about you.

It won't matter what she does if you don't fix your own mess. It won't matter what new toys you buy, yes even that awesome new car you want, if you don't take care of what is going on inside your soul.

Too often I hear men who just stick to the story that only when their wives change will things get better, only when their wives do what the men want will the men be able to really achieve.

That's just plain not true. Not only is it not true, but thinking that way will actually cause even more problems in your relationship, because now you have placed the burden of your change and growth on her shoulders and that is beyond unfair to do to her.

She can't change you for you, she can't make your choices for you, she can't do your work for you, she can't do any of that. So if you're putting this on her, things will only get worse. If you have done that, or if you are doing that, Stop. Just Stop.

Own your reality. Own your relationship. Own your life today. Think about every area in your relationship that is not where you want it to be and consider what you can do, starting today, to improve that area. Take action in each area. Call her more. Text her more. Date her more. Become the man she desires to have in her life.

As you start to make changes, you will see her attitude and response to you change as well. As you start to own your situation and as you start to do the work, you will notice her language and interactions with you change as well.

It won't be easy. There will be resistance. She might question your motives. If you have not done this before, if you have been the sort of husband who has been putting the burden of the relationship on her, you should expect her to wonder what is going on and even to question if this is a real change or some sort of temporary thing you're doing.

Stay the course though. Work through the challenges. Become the man who comes out of the other side of the tunnel with a new reality.

It is possible. You can have that life. You can have that relationship with your wife. You can be the man whose wife looks at him with those alluring eyes from across the room. You can be the man who the other guys look at with jealousy when they see you with your wife.

It's not about her, it all starts with you.

Forty-Eight
IT IS ABOUT HER

This time I'm going to the other side of the discussion from the last chapter. Here we are talking about her, instead of you. If you skipped it, please go back and read the last chapter, It's Not About Her.

Often when I'm talking with the guys and we get into the conversation where I discuss that it isn't about her, and that it is about you, as the man, stepping up and doing your part in the relationship, I get push back. I get comments about what she should do, what she needs to do, how she needs to change, what she needs to understand, and on and on.

And you know what guys? You're absolutely right! As I mentioned earlier, she does have to make other choices, she does have to evolve, and she does have to change, just as you do. She does need to spend time understanding you, just as you need to spend time understanding her. That is the exact reason that I hold the occasional event for women, helping them to see the other side, helping them to understand our struggles, our challenges, and our perspectives as men.

Those events are great, I've had women tell me they were relationship changers, and I love hearing that feedback... but that still isn't what we're talking about here.

You see this book is for us men, it's about you and me and our journey towards becoming more significant men. It is about our side of the equation, and this chapter is all about her. I'm going to write here as if you are married, but the same points apply to men who are dating or who wish to be.

Let me ask you a serious question. When was the last time you actually talked with your wife on a deep level and asked her deep questions? In other words, when was the last time you talked with her about something so significant and serious that the outcome of the conversation could change the course of your entire relationship?

If you're like most guys, the honest answer to this is never. Most men have never had that level of conversation with their wives. First, because it isn't in the nature of most men to have those sorts of conversations. Second, because most guys are not willing to drop their masks or come out of their fortresses and potentially open their hearts to getting crushed. Third, most men have no idea what questions to ask or what to talk about in such a conversation.

If you want the relationship that a significant man has, if you truly want to get to that level, you have to have these conversations. The following are some of the questions I would challenge you to ask her. As a very important point here, when you do ask these questions, shut up and listen! Let her know that you really want to understand and even take notes if you have to. During this time, while you are asking her these questions and listening to her answers, do not offer any solutions, answers, justifications, or explanations. Just listen…

Here are some questions you can use. Just replace "honey" with whatever you call your wife.

- Honey, what does it mean, to you, to have security in your life?
- Honey, what does it feel like, to you, to have me desire you?
- Honey, what does my love, for you, actually mean to you?
- Honey, what is a dream you had that has fallen away in our busy lives?
- Honey, what does it feel like, to you, knowing that I'm providing for our family?

- Honey, what does it feel like to you to have a meaningful relationship with me?
- Honey, if there was one thing you wish was different in our relationship, what would it be? …and lastly, and guys if you're able to get to these last two, really listen:
- Honey, what does it mean to you to see me succeed as your husband?
- Honey, what does it mean to you to see me succeed as a man?

Guys notice that in questions like these, which are all critically important (although the exact wording of the conversation and questions would change for you and your wife's way of speaking), that the language is about her feelings and what these things mean to her.

That's really important.

When you have this conversation, it is all about her. It is about her hopes, her dreams, and her desires. It is about what she is feeling. It is about what she is looking for in the future.

Your job during this discussion is not to offer advice or answers, even though they will immediately come into your mind right then (because that is what us men do). Your job is to listen, it is to really look at her and see her, and it is to focus on what she is saying.

While she is talking, look at her, I mean really look at her. Notice her hair, notice her eyes, notice her moods and expressions, notice her. When she is telling you about a dream that has fallen away, look at her and listen.

Does she look sad or does she look hopeful? Is there sorrow in her eyes? Is there hope in her eyes?

Remember when you were dating, and you noticed all that, do you remember your queen? You noticed her expressions, you noticed her hair, her eyes, you could see her dreams and her hopes in not only what she said, but also how she said it.

Get back to that place.

It is all about her. And then, after this conversation, it is about you getting to work, because you are her husband. This is your job; this is your responsibility.

You owe it to her and to yourself to follow through. Far too many men have let this part die, and their relationships are dying right alongside.

You have to step up and do the work if you want to have the amazing relationship with her. If you want her to look at you "that way" again, then you need to start seeing her "that way" again.

Now I know that the vast majority of men who read this won't choose to do the work. They will not come out of their fortress and will not drop the mask. That makes me sad, but it is reality.

I also know that for those who do choose to take the risk and do the work, that they will be taking a massive step forward in their relationship. I know that those men who are willing to be open are the men who get to that level. I know that those men will have a connection with their wives that most other men will never experience or understand. I know that those men will have a powerful life partner, one who lifts them, encourages them, and supports them through their challenges. I know that those men will have wives looking at them with pride.

Which will you choose to become?

Forty-Nine
PROTECTING YOUR DAUGHTERS

This chapter won't be an easy read, and it won't be exactly like the others. However, this could end up being the single most important chapter in this entire book, it is that critical.

Men, instinctively you know that it is your job to protect your family and your daughters. You know that it is your job to make sure that your girls are not in danger. You know that it is your job to protect your daughters from harm.

This seems obvious with the normal things we tend to think about. We know that we want to keep our daughters safe, we want to physically protect them from boys and men who might abuse them, and we feel the instinct to show up powerfully to anyone who threatens our little girls. As men, we know that if some jerk lays a hand on our precious daughter he will have to answer to us.

Even writing this now, as a father of daughters, the very idea that someone might pose a risk to them is making my heart race a bit faster. I know, exactly as many of you fathers know, that I will crawl over burning glass to protect my family and my daughters.

However, there is a danger lurking and brewing under the surface. Something that far too many fathers are turning a blind eye towards. Something that far too many are pretending is not an issue.

That issue is the impact that the culture of hardcore porn is having on our children. Yes, we can relate to our kids having to deal with peer pressure, we can relate to our kids having to make decisions about who to be friends with, about drinking, smoking, and drugs, we can relate to all of that.

However, we never had to deal with a culture where girls, little girls even 7 or 8 years old, are growing up in a world that is so heavily influenced by hardcore porn (and where that influence is growing). My heart breaks for what girls have shared about the world that they are growing up in and what they are learning.

These girls, like your daughter, are learning that they are expected to perform acts that hurt them. These girls are learning that they are expected to engage in activities that leave them scared, confused, wounded, and feeling alone. These girls are learning that they are supposed to give the boy anything he asks for.

This is a direct assault on girls. Sexual bullying and sexual pressure has become nearly a daily occurrence for millions of girls, young girls just like your daughters and mine.

The following will passages not be easy to read, but as mentioned earlier, this is critical for you to understand. Here are some key quotes (from an important article written by Melinda Tankard Reist, called *Growing Up in Pornland: Girls Have Had it with Porn Conditioned Boys* *) you need to really take in and think about:

"Some see sex only in terms of *performance*, where what counts most is the boy enjoying it. I asked a 15–year–old about her first sexual experience. She replied: "I think my body looked OK. He seemed to enjoy it". Many girls seem cut off from their own sense of pleasure or intimacy. That *he* enjoyed it is the main thing. Girls and young women are under a lot of pressure to give boys and men what they want, to adopt pornified roles and behaviors, with their bodies being merely sex aids. Growing up in a pornified landscape, girls learn that they are service stations for male gratification and pleasure."

"Asked "How do you know a guy likes you?," an 8–year–old girl replied: "He still wants to talk to you after you suck him off." A male high school student said to a girl: "If you suck my dick I'll give you a kiss." Girls are expected to provide sex acts for tokens of affection. A 15–year–old told me she didn't enjoy sex at all, but that getting it out of the way quickly was the only way her boyfriend would settle down and watch a movie with her."

"I'm increasingly seeing 7–year–old girls who seek help on what to do about requests for naked images. Being asked "send me a picture of your tits" is an almost daily occurrence for many. "How do I say 'no' without hurting his feelings"? girls ask."

"7–year–old girls ask me questions about bondage and S&M. They ask, if he wants to hit me, tie me up and stalk me, does that mean he loves me? Girls are putting up with demeaning and disrespectful behaviors, and thereby internalizing pornography's messages about their submissive role."

"Some girls suffer physical injury from porn–inspired sexual acts, including anal sex. The director of a domestic violence center wrote to me a couple of years ago about the increase in porn–related injuries to girls aged 14 and up, from acts including torture."

"The proliferation and globalization of hypersexualized imagery and pornographic themes makes healthy sexual exploration almost impossible. Sexual conquest and domination are untempered by the bounds of respect, intimacy and authentic human connection. Young people are not learning about intimacy, friendship and love, but about cruelty and humiliation."

If the quotes above are making you a combination of heart broken, outraged, sad, and really angry, good. They should, they better. This is a tiny glimpse into the world your daughter and her friends are dealing with right now, today. This is her world, this is the culture she is experiencing, and this is the situation she is trying to navigate through. This should make you sad, and it should make you livid.

Your daughters are growing up in a culture where they do not even expect tenderness, they do not even consider the idea of intimacy that isn't sexual, they cannot imagine a slow building of suspense of what might be in the future if the relationship continues, they simply have no concept of any of that side of sexuality. They would not even understand what it means to "make love", as love is not part of the pornified world they are growing up in.

Sex for girls today, growing up in a world of porn, is completely disassociated from love in every aspect. Your daughter is growing up in a world where love has been entirely removed from the equation.

Now, here is where it gets tough for you. It is one thing to become aware of this. It is another to act. Becoming a significant man requires action; it is not enough for you to learn.

Are you talking with your daughters about this? Clearly, you do not need to talk with them about the mechanics of sex, they know what goes where and how things work, so you probably don't need to talk about the birds and the bees.

This isn't about using condoms and the conversation about safe sex, as important as that is. This is talking about something that is even more serious, because this is going to the soul of who she is becoming as a woman.

You do need to talk to your daughter. You need to do this; this is not a conversation for you to leave to your wife. This is your responsibility. Your daughter needs to hear this from you, in your words, as her father.

As her father, she has to hear you tell her these things. Your voice has incredible power in this conversation, no other voice that can substitute for yours. You have to talk with her about the relationship between love and sex; how they are different and connected at the same time. You have to talk with her about respect. You have to talk with her about modesty. You have to talk with her and explain why it is that what the boys are asking for isn't right. You have to talk with her about what to do when a boy asks her to send him nude pics of herself. You have to talk with her about what to do when she is pressured into doing something physically that she is not comfortable doing.

If those last ones got you, they better. Because despite what you might think, she may have already received that text request or been asked to do things she doesn't want to do, and she is all alone trying to figure out how to answer or what to do.

In many schools if she doesn't go along with what the boy asks, she will then have to deal with the insults, the taunting, the bullying, the social media threats, and more that goes along with this issue. And again, if this issue has never been discussed in your home, she will feel like she has to deal with this all alone, with no one by her side, not even her own father. You need to be her rock; she needs to know that you will go to the ends of the Earth to protect her.

Nearly every father who learns about what his daughter is involved in and what she is dealing with begins with a denial. Most fathers of the girls who are involved in this assume that their daughters are not, and so those same fathers are caught off guard when their daughter is the one who gets hurt.

You have to have this conversation. You have to let her know that saying no to a boy is ok. You have to let her know it is ok even if it hurts his feelings; if he is asking for stuff like that go ahead and hurt his feelings for crying out loud!

You have to let her know that you think she is beautiful, as she is. You have to let her know that you think she is amazing, as she is. You have to let her know that you think she is powerful, as she is. You have to let her know that you are aware of the world she is growing up in, and that you will always provide her a safe place. This has to come directly from your voice, as her father.

You see gentlemen, you may have locked all the doors and windows in your house, but your daughter could be experiencing a life–changing attack right now. This attack could be taking place today, under your watch. As you are reading this, she could be in her room, or at a friend's house, or even at school, trying to figure out how to deal with this assault.

You cannot leave her vulnerable to this attack; you must step up and arm her with your words, your wisdom, and your presence. If you are a father of a daughter, this is not an option—you must protect her.

* Referenced article can be found here: http://www.abc.net. au/religion/ articles/2016/03/07/4420147.htm

Fifty
LIFTING YOUR SONS

*I*f you thought I might lighten up a bit after that last chapter, I'm not. This time we are going to the other side of the equation, and we are going to talk about our sons. This is, as the last chapter was, critically important for you to take very seriously.

What boys today are learning, including your son and mine, from the influence of sex and porn on the society is damaging them on multiple levels. Boys, just like our sons, are growing up in a world where the expectation of porn–like sex is what many consider normal.

Think about the visual world that your son is growing up in. Movies, television, billboards, magazines, video games, burger joints, online, offline; everywhere is selling everything and anything with sex. Your son is already visually attracted to these images, even when he is far too young to have any idea why. He sees sexualized women in everything, all day long.

The average age today for boys' first encounter with porn (not just an image of a naked woman, but real hardcore pornography) has lowered to about 11–12 years old. That's just the average age, many start when they are 6 or 7 years old. That also happens to be close to the average age that boys get a smartphone with Internet access.

Boys now have porn available on their mobile devices and they can view it 24/7, with ease. In the past boys had to find an adult magazine or sneak a peek at an adult video. Those actions carried some degree of risk for him; there was some thought that he might be found and get in trouble for possessing porn.

Today that barrier is gone. There is no more sneaking around. There is no more hiding a magazine. There is none of that and no risk. Today boys can access anything they want to see with a few searches. It is there to see, all the time, no credit card needed.

What boys, like your son, are finding isn't the "soft" sort of images like a topless woman or even a fully naked woman posing on a beach. Those kinds of images seem quaint and old-fashioned these days.

This is why Playboy has stopped publishing magazines with naked women. Images of naked women no longer were enough, porn has moved to video and porn has continued to move into more and more hardcore acts.

What your son will find when he searches is hardcore pornography, continuously darker and more perverse. He will see sexual acts that you never even consider as a grown man. He will see women treated in unspeakable ways. He will see that women are there to please men, and little more. He will see and learn that violence towards women is ok, if the man gets what he wants.

Since boys model behavior based on what they see, it is no stretch at all to realize that boys will expect sex to be what they see in porn. They will act the way they see men act in porn. They will talk the way men talk in porn. They will expect girls to act like the women they see in porn. They base their entire view of the sexual interaction between men and women on what they see in porn.

In the porn that your son is watching, his view of sexual relationships takes shape. Young boys (again most start seeing this before they are teenagers) have very fluid brains, and porn is having a serious impact on their ability to grow or keep any kind of focus on any single girl.

If you have a son, you already know that he is naturally distracted, constantly moving from idea to idea, bouncing from chair to chair. With porn, he is also learning that he needs to be constantly moving from one girl to another, seeking new ways to be stimulated.

Considering that his male nature will give him the go ahead, he desperately needs you to work with him, teach him, train him, and keep him on the right path. Porn is like pouring gasoline on his fire, and he needs you to put that fire out, he will not be capable of doing so himself.

As a father, one of the most important lessons for you to teach your son is that he is responsible for controlling himself. It is his job to learn about himself, and to manage his inclinations. He is not an animal, and just as you teach him that he can't jump from one couch to another, without breaking the couches; you need to teach him that he cannot jump from one girl to another, without breaking the girls. His mind will naturally lead him towards jumping around, and you have to lead him back to solid ground.

The constant stream of videos and images, the constant increase in the level of explicit acts that he watches, makes it harder and harder for him back in the real world. With porn as the way he learns about sex and relationships, where is the romance? Where is the love? Where is the connection? Where is the tenderness? Where is the seduction? Where is any of that?

Of course that is all missing, because none of that sells, so he may never know those things even exist in a healthy sexual relationship.

Consider as well that the primary mode of communication for kids today is texting. Rarely is there an actual phone call, just text messages. Text messages are simple and safe; he can ignore them, and they're not in real-time, like an in-person conversation is. So think about all that, and then think about the following scenario:

Your young son, who already prefers text messages, is ready to maybe go on a date. So he could build up the courage to maybe walk up to and ask some girls out on dates. After he does that, he then has to deal with the various rejections from the girls who don't want to go out with him. After he does that, he then has to work to save up and use his money on the date. After he does that, he then might get a kiss good night at the end of the date... Or, he could close the door to his bedroom and have instant access to a never–ending stream of videos and images that he could use to gratify himself, without any risk, cost, or difficulty. This exact scenario is what teenage boys are dealing with, right now. Your son may be struggling with this exact scenario, right now.

This grows into a bigger problem, as he begins to have serious challenges in creating and keeping a relationship with an actual real girl. The girl who doesn't look and act like a porn star, because no woman in real life looks and acts like a porn star.

Boys are actually starting to say that they aren't even interested in building relationships with real girls, because there is too much hassle, too much risk and rejection, and not enough variety and desire. The longer that boys use porn to satisfy themselves, the more challenging it will be for them to connect with a real girl, and ultimately a real woman.

Think about these quotes from Belinda Luscombe in an article titled, *Porn and the Threat to Virility* *:

"A growing number of young men are convinced that their sexual responses have been sabotaged because their brains were virtually marinated in porn when they were adolescents. Their generation has consumed explicit content in quantities and varieties never before possible, on devices designed to deliver content swiftly and privately, all at an age when their brains were more plastic—more prone to permanent change—than in later life. These young men feel like unwitting guinea pigs in a largely unmonitored decade–long experiment in sexual conditioning."

"After a while, he says, those videos did not arouse him as much, so he moved on to different configurations, sometimes involving just women, sometimes one woman and several guys, sometimes even an unwilling woman. "I could find anything I imagined and a lot of stuff I couldn't imagine," he says. After the appeal of those waned, he moved on to the next level, more intense, often more violent."

"He had an opportunity to have actual sex, with a real partner. He was attracted to her and she to him, as demonstrated by the fact that she was naked in her bedroom in front of him. But his body didn't seem to be interested. "There was a disconnect between what I wanted in my mind and how my body reacted," he says. He simply couldn't get the necessary hydraulics going."

"Porn was as much a part of adolescence as homework or acne. "It was normal and it was everywhere," he says. He grew up in an era when what used to be considered X–rated was becoming mainstream, and he and his friends used to watch explicit videos constantly, he says, even during class, on their school–issued laptops."

"Most young women … are not immune to the effects of growing up in a culture rife with this content. Teen girls increasingly report that guys are expecting them to behave like porn starlets, encumbered by neither body hair nor sexual needs of their own."

As researchers dig deeper on the impact of porn on the brain, consider these two quotes from Gary Wilson, the author of *Your Brain on Porn*:

"Porn trains your brain to need everything associated with porn to get aroused," Wilson says. That includes not only the content but also the delivery method. Because porn videos are limitless, free and fast, users can click to a whole new scene or genre as soon as their arousal ebbs and thereby, says Wilson, "condition their arousal patterns to ongoing, ever changing novelty."

"The result in some Internet porn users is higher brain activation to internet porn, and less arousal to sex with a real person," Wilson argues. And then there's habituation: the need for more to get the same hit. "Extreme novelty, certain fetishes, shock and surprise and anxiety–all those elevate dopamine," he says. "So they need those to be sexually aroused."

The easily available hardcore porn of today is literally rewiring your son's brain. The impact of internet porn on boy's brains is severe, with their brains reacting and changing the same way a heroin addict's brain does. The boy who grows up viewing this porn is having his brain rewired like that heroin addict, he will continuously need more and more, and he will need more and more intense videos to satisfy his brain. It becomes a very dark and difficult circle for him, one he'll have a very hard time escaping.

This is a very big deal, and you can't make light of it. This isn't a time to joke about boys being boys, or how you have seen porn in your life and you're ok. Your son is being used as the guinea pig in the experiment, with the result being his inability to have a healthy sexual relationship with his own wife when he is a man.

You teach your son about the harmful impact that drugs will have on him, and you need to teach him about the harmful impact that porn will as well. It won't be easy. But, you didn't become a father to take the easy way out. Just as you are on a journey to become a significant man—so too is your son, and he needs you as the guide on his journey.

Part of your job in raising and lifting your son up is to teach him about things like honor, respect, love, virtue, and modesty. Part of your job, in teaching your son, is to teach him about what marriage is like, what the relationship with his wife will and can be.

Just like in the conversation with your daughter, you probably don't need to have the birds and the bees talk about mechanics and what goes where. Your son has likely known all that for a while; you're talking about the other issues, these issues that will shape him as a man.

Lifting your son up as a young man who knows about honoring himself and honoring women, as someone who respects himself and women, as someone who understands and appreciates modesty, as someone who sees the benefits in virtue, that is how you will know you are doing your job as a father.

A young man who raised like that and who lives like that will have a much easier time with his entire life, and he will stand out as an exceptional man of character. He will already be on his own path towards becoming a significant man. He will be the young man that women notice and that other men will turn to. Simply because you took this issue as seriously as it was and you were willing to lift him up in a way that few other men will do.

Gentlemen, you know how important a positive sex life is to you as a man, you know how life–giving and valuable that truly is, and you know how much that impacts your entire world. If your son grows up and is not taught the truth about these issues, if he grows up thinking porn's example is how he should interact with his wife, then your son is going to live a lifetime of dysfunction in his bedroom and be unable to have a healthy intimate connection.

Lift up your son; be there for him. You need to know that he is going to face, if he has not already, serious peer pressure on this issue. He will be in situations, often, where he is going to have to make his own choice. He will face times when he might be the only boy in the entire school who is not ok with asking girls for nude pictures. He might be the only boy anyone knows who doesn't think it is ok to have sex with as many girls as possible. He might be the only boy who doesn't think it is ok to just use girls and dump them that night. Other kids might bully him, say he doesn't like girls, or threaten and harass him on social media, all because he is trying to stand up and be a young man of character.

You need to know that he may be facing these attacks; he may be dealing with this right now. Again, lift him up, and be there for him. Let him know how proud you are of him. Let him know how strong he is being. Let him know how courageous he is being. Let him know that you love him. In your words, he needs to hear those things from you; no one else can speak to him the way you can speak to him.

The world of today is tough for your son. You have the opportunity to provide him with a safe place to rest and learn while he is growing and facing the world. Empower him on his journey of manhood, and welcome him, with open arms, anytime he needs you.

* Referenced article can be found here: http://time.com/4277510/porn-and-the-threat-to-virility/

Fifty-One
ANGRY WITH GOD

Not long ago a teenage friend of our family died suddenly in a car accident. That is the hardest kind of death to deal with, when it seems so random, without any explanation, and when it happens to a young person entering the prime of their life.

It is a natural feeling to be angry at times like that. It is a natural question to ask why. Although there is no comforting answer to the why question I can offer, because I do not speak for God, I do want to share my thoughts on the anger part.

As you know, I'm a Christian man, my faith is a major cornerstone of who I am and what I believe. I have often been asked if I am a pastor, since I share these ideas openly and discuss these issues with many people (the answer is no, I'm not a pastor, although it has crossed my mind over the years).

As a Christian, these are the times when that natural response of anger can be "questioned". I put that in quotes because there are many who insist that we should never be angry, as men in general, and that we should never be angry with God.

I'm telling you now that not only is it ok to be angry as a man, from time to time, but it is also ok to be angry with God.

Don't worry, He is big enough to handle your anger, I promise.

In fact, I would go further and even suggest that if you have never been angry with God, you have not yet experienced the full relationship that you can have with Him.

If you never allow yourself to be angry with God, you are in essence trying to hide part of yourself from Him. Which doesn't work too well, since He knows anyway.

Think about it like this:

Imagine you're upset with your wife. There has been some issue building for a long time, a disagreement that has been going back and forth for months. And now you're angry, really angry.

What are your choices? On one hand, you can pretend that you're not upset and that you're not angry. You can hold that all inside hidden from her and let that anger fester until it turns into resentment down the road. On the other hand, you can express your anger and get it out in the open so that there are no uncertain terms about how you feel.

Now your wife has that information, the good and the bad, she knows how you feel and the two of you can work through whatever the issue was.

What if you never told her and you never let her know how angry you were? Then you keep that all inside, where it grows into much more negative and poisonous thoughts. As mentioned, there is even risk that it grows into serious resentment, which is often be fatal to a relationship.

At the bare minimum, if you don't tell her, you have to hide that part of you from her, you have to make sure you never let her see your true feelings about that issue. So you have either an issue you're hiding or an issue that turns into resentment (neither of which are good), all because you refused to let your anger exist in that conversation.

Think about this now in the context of God. If you are angry with him, tell Him. Do not try to hide that from Him. He already knows anyway, and again yes, He can handle it.

In fact, He wants to hear it from you. He wants to hear the full range of your life; He wants to hear you talk with Him about how you really feel.

So let it all out. Be angry.

What you can't do however, is let that anger turn into bitterness or a feeling of being a victim or letting the anger turn into a grudge. That is not healthy for you in any scenario.

So go ahead and be angry with God, tell him exactly how you feel, let Him into that part of your heart as well. Scream, yell, and cry, whatever you have to do.

Trust Him with your thoughts, all of them.

Once you have, once you have let out everything you have inside, you've entered an important time, because that is when you have to move on to the next part of your relationship.

You see it is one thing to feel angry with God and to express that anger to Him. It is another thing entirely to hang onto that anger after you have let it all out and shared it all with Him. You have to move on from that pain and that anger; you cannot let the anger build. You have to grow past that and into a positive place.

Think about part of the story of David, from the Bible. David's baby has just died, and this was after David had been faithfully praying and fasting for his child's health. When the baby died, David went to worship God, knowing where the child now was and knowing that the child was with God.

God knows your pain, He hears your cries, He understands how hard and difficult life can be, and He wants you to share all of you with Him.

But like David, we can't remain there in pain, and we can't remain in anger. We share our grief and anger with Him, and let Him work through us. If we let Him help us, and if we are willing to open our hearts, we may learn things we never have considered before.

Trust Him with your anger, and let Him work through your challenge with you.

PS—It should go without saying, but I want to be very clear here. I'm talking about anger, the emotion we all feel from time to time. I'm not talking about violence, not talking about screaming, abusive language, nothing like that… violence and abuse towards anyone (including yourself) is never ok.

Fifty-Two
UNTIL YOU DO THIS, YOU'LL BE STUCK

When I talk with a man about what is holding him back, we start with the common answers like the poor economy, he doesn't have the right degree, his wife doesn't believe in him, he says he doesn't have enough money, and so on. All those are the excuses, but none of them is the real core issue, the real answer as to what is holding him back.

Then, after we've gone through those surface and easy answers, we eventually get to the right place, and he is willing to say it: *he* is what is holding him back. He finally acknowledges that he is really the biggest obstacle in his way.

No matter how much you may want to find someone else or something else to blame, the reality is that you are the one in your own way, more than everything else combined is.

This was the truth for me too. For the longest time, as I was trying to figure things out, it took me a while to identify the common denominator—me! Yep what is now blatantly obvious is that I was in my own way. I'm confident saying that is the same answer for you.

You are the person that is in your way. Your current mindset is holding you back. Your lack of a skillset is holding you back. Your decisions are holding you back. Your choice to let life happen to you instead of creating and executing a battle plan is holding you back.

I'm willing to guess that if you're the kind of man who is reading the messages in this book, then you're ready to accept this truth, or somewhere down in your gut you already know this is true, even if you have never really wanted to come face–to–face with that truth.

Here is what you have to do. And until you do this, you'll be stuck.

You'll be stuck at your income level, you'll be stuck in your relationship with your wife, you'll be stuck in leading your kids, you'll be stuck in your connection to God, in every area you'll be stuck.

Quite simply, the solution is in your choices and your actions. The actual process of making a choice is where most men stop. Even though it seems odd that most stop there that is unfortunately the reality for the majority of men. Most men are content to stay where they are and then complain about what they don't have instead of choosing and getting started.

Choose something and get started. It sounds simple, and it is. You simply need to choose different things for your future than you did for your past.

Quite literally, choose something, make a decision, and start taking action. Yes, it is that simple. Don't over think this. Don't over–analyze this. Don't paralyze yourself and sabotage yourself by examining every option. Choose and then act.

You want to earn more money over the next year? Awesome, what exactly are you going to do differently to get there? OK good, get started doing that. You have too many ideas? OK, then choose one, anyone, and get started doing that.

Here is a secret that high achieving men already know. You get to choose again, and again, and again. You're not tied to that decision for the rest of the life, if you are willing to keep learning and willing to keep choosing.

For too many, they become stuck right where they are. The choices sometimes seem overpowering with too many options to consider. What happens then is instead of choosing, there is paralysis.

That was the truth for me too. When I was down and hurting, and knew that I wanted more, knew that I was here on Earth for more, I had too many ideas, too many businesses I was interested in starting, too many investments I wanted to make, too many opportunities to create or pursue.

I was frozen. I was looking at the choices, and spending way too much time trying to figure out which one was right. There I was, the man who didn't choose any one thing over the fear of choosing the wrong thing.

My life began to turn around when I realized the power of my choices and that it was OK for me to choose something that didn't work out, and then choose something else that did. Between losing everything and my work now, I was involved in about a dozen other businesses of one form or another. Some as a silent investor, some as a partner, some as an active owner. Until I finally got to the real work God called me to do, I was choosing all sorts of wrong things! But, I kept going, kept choosing, kept failing and getting back up.

And guess what? You get to change too. If you make a choice and it turns out to not work the way you wanted, then you get to make another choice, and then another, and another.

Soon you'll find that all those choices have helped you to fine–tune exactly what it is that you really do want and the life you really do want to live. You can fine–tune your business and income with your choices, you can fine–tune your marriage with your choices, and the same is true in leading your children, or your fitness, or your faith, and every other area of your life.

Which means that not only are you getting yourself unstuck by choosing and starting, you are actually putting yourself on the path to living the life of significance that you want to live.

Will there be work? Of course, you know that. Will there be challenge? Absolutely, and you know that too. You know there isn't any magic system that will simply give you the life you want at the click of a mouse, you're smarter than that.

To make this practical, think about one of the major issues you have been dealing with. Something in your finances, relationships, faith, anything, look at your options and pick one…

… then stop analyzing the situation, make a choice to do something different and start doing it.

Fifty-Three
MAYBE YOU SHOULD JUST QUIT

Yes, you're right. It's too hard. There are too many obstacles. You don't get the support you need from your wife. Your friends don't understand what you're trying to do. Your family thinks you're crazy.

It costs too much. You can't afford it. The mentoring you want is out of your league. You should probably leave the opportunity to other men who are more qualified that you.

Maybe you should just quit after all.

That's what it seems like the world is telling you anyway. All you hear are reasons why you shouldn't do it. Reasons why you shouldn't open your own business. Reasons why you shouldn't hire a mentor. Reasons why you shouldn't become a coach. Reasons why you shouldn't be a leader. Reasons why you shouldn't follow your dreams.

What if you fail? What if it doesn't turn out how you wanted? What if you lose everything?

Yes, you're right. It's too risky. There is no certain path. There is no sure thing.

Maybe you should just quit after all.

Quitting sure is the easier thing to do. People will nod and understand, they won't judge you, they'll agree with your decision. They will even reinforce your choice to quit, telling you that you made the right decision. They will tell you that it is better for you to be safe than sorry.

Because they quit before too, and they will welcome you into the club of quitters. They will be happy to have you there in the club, the more the merrier.

If you think I'm being harsh here, I'm not. This is simply the truth.

The reason so many don't want you to change, and do want you to quit is because that is the path they took, that is where their journey took them. They want validation for their own choice to quit, or to have never tried in the first place.

If you push past and you refuse to quit, your success shines a light on their failures or, at a minimum, their choice to quit. I've shared other related thoughts on this earlier in the book.

If you don't quit, if you work through the challenges, if you solve the problems, if you overcome the obstacles, you are showing the entire world that there is another way. You are showing your friends, your family, your wife, and—most importantly—yourself that there is another way.

But it's hard. That's true.

You are likely to fall down. You are likely to get hurt. You are likely to feel pain. You are likely to invest in yourself in ways you have never done before. You are likely to be pushed and challenged, asked to go to places you never thought of in your entire life…

… and that scares most men away from the entire idea of living a significant life.

Most men don't want to actually walk the walk to get there.

Oh, they will talk about it all right; there is always plenty of talk to go around. However, when it comes to walking the walk, when it comes to opening up and going deep on the real issues and struggles that men have, the majority close up and choose not to change.

In other words, most men quit. They quit doing anything they need to do in order to become a significant man, they quit investing, they quit growing, they quit taking the steps they have to take to move forward, and they quit taking daily action to create the life they want to live.

For a while, they might keep on talking the talk, but that ends up fading away as well. It takes too much energy to keep up that image over time, and they slither away back into the darkness, unwilling to come out into the light.

You can choose another way. You can choose to fight; you can choose to get into the battle of your life. You can choose not to be the man dying on your deathbed wondering, "What if I didn't quit, all those years ago? What if I really would have just chosen to live the life I was created to live?"

Yes, fighting for yourself might hurt, maybe even lots. Yes, fighting for the life you want to live will cost you; it will not be overnight, it will not be safe, and it will not be easy. But, wow is it worth it!

I'm a big time movie fan, and I'm going to share a great Braveheart scene here. Think about this as it relates to your life, to your battle, and to what you are facing today:

William Wallace: I AM William Wallace! And I see a whole army of my countrymen, here in defiance of tyranny. You've come to fight as free men... and free men you are. What will you do with that freedom? Will you fight?

Soldier: Fight? Against that? No. We will run. And we will live.

William Wallace: Aye, fight and you may die. Run, and you'll live... at least a while. And, dying in your beds, many years from now, would you be willing to trade ALL the days, from this day to that, for one chance, just one chance, to come back here and tell our enemies that they may take our lives, but they'll never take... OUR FREEDOM!

If you're like me, this scene gives you chills. It gave me chills just typing it. It does because we both know that, way down in our souls, that real freedom is what we are made for. It scares us, but we know it is true.

As you might have noticed in this book, in these chapters, one of the recurring themes is about choice. Here we are yet again.

You have a choice to make, about quitting, when you are becoming a significant man.

Will you listen to your critics, will you retreat under the pressure and quit? Or will you choose to not take the easy way out, will you fight through to become more? Will you choose to make sure they never take your freedom?

As always, the choice is yours.

Fifty-Four

PAIN OR SUFFERING?

What is pain? What is suffering? Why do we experience pain? Why do we experience suffering?

Did you know that these two, pain and suffering, are actually different things?

It might sound like these are trivial questions, or asking semantics questions, but they are not. Learning to distinguish the difference between pain and suffering is one of the most important aspects to living a significant life.

We will all experience pain, every single one of us. And, we don't need to do the manly thing and start comparing our levels of pain against one another. There is no contest with pain. All of us are going to deal with pain, on and off, during our entire lives.

That is simply the reality of being alive.

I don't care if your pain is greater than mine, and you should not care if my pain is greater than yours. Our entire society has become too focused on comparison, and with guys we tend to compete on everything, even pain. Let's stop that. That competition is beyond pointless. Competing on levels of pain simply does not matter.

What is pain anyway? On the surface, we know the answer to this, we touch our hand to a hot stove, and there is pain.

Pain, as in physical pain, has very specific attributes. We know the biology side well; think of the hot stove example. We touch the stove and our nervous system sends the signal to our brain that something is not right, and we react. We quickly pull our hand away from the source of our pain.

However, when we move from pain to suffering, we have moved from the biology side towards the psychology side of pain, and this is the sort of impact that can linger long after the biological pain is over. Years or decades later, we can still feel the impact of these wounds.

Suffering is when we engage in self–talk, when we create beliefs about others and ourselves in our own minds. Suffering is a result of the emotional and the mental response we have from our pain.

Depending on what sort of conversation we have, in our minds, after the pain has taken place is the direct link to what level of suffering we experience in our lives. The internal conversations and expectations we create for ourselves become the main drivers of our suffering.

Pain is going to happen; there is nothing you can do to stop pain from taking place. You cannot stop it for you, you cannot stop it for your spouse, you cannot stop it for your children; you cannot stop it for anyone on Earth.

The question then becomes, what do you do with this knowledge? How does knowing this have a practical impact on your life?

Before moving into that, I want to step back to one of the books that has had a profound impact on who I am, what I believe, and how I view the concepts of pain and suffering.

The book is *Man's Search For Meaning*, by Viktor Frankl. I recommend this book to anyone and everyone who has even the slightest interest in living a better, happier, and more significant life. For the men I directly mentor, this book is required reading. It is not a long book, it is not an expensive book, and it is a life–changing book, so go get it.

In Dr. Frankl's book, he wrote about the impacts on his life, as a prisoner, in the Nazi concentration camps of World War II. In the camps his pregnant wife, his brother, his mother, and his father were all murdered. He describes how the Nazi captors and guards took away every element of humanity, and he tells these stories in detail that is difficult to read at times, but important to read at the same time.

He discusses how there was only one thing the Nazis could not take from him: his own choice as to how he was going to respond to what was taking place. They could murder his family, strip him naked, shave him bald, take away his name, degrade him, deprive him, torture him, and put him through horrific realities that no human should ever face.

However, during all of that, during everything that is happening to him, he could hold onto his own choice about how he is going to react to all of that. He can choose. He can decide. He is the one who will choose to make the shift (or not) from pain to suffering.

If there was ever a person to fall into the suffering statements, such as "This is not fair!", "Why is this happening to me?", "I deserve better than this!", "I can't take anymore.", "What have I done to deserve this?" it was Dr. Frankl, and all the other prisoners of the concentration camps.

What he chose was something that required strength, required faith, and required serious thought. He made a conscious choice about how he was going to react; because that was the one thing the Nazis could not ever take from him. No one can take your ability to choose how to act and react.

You cannot control what will happen to you in this life, but you can control how you will react to what happens to you. (That is a line my kids have heard me repeat over and over to them.)

It is a similar choice we get to make every time there is pain in our lives. Of course, we pray never to be in a situation like what Dr. Frankl experienced, and we pray that never happens again to any human.

The perspective is important and powerful, however. If he could make that choice, during the most horrific time in human history, don't you think you can with your current challenges? (Please note, I am not comparing his pain to yours or mine, I am bringing up his experience to illustrate this point.)

So how do we use this concept in becoming a significant man? Where do we go from here?

The first thing to realize, and accept, is that you will experience pain in your life. There is zero point in fighting that reality, know it. The second thing is to realize that you get to decide how you are going to react to that pain, and you get to decide if you are going to move from pain to suffering.

What you cannot do is ignore it.

As men we often hear, and we'll even say this to ourselves, in our own minds, that we should ignore the pain and simply man up.

Now I'm not the kind of guy to totally dismiss that concept. I think men should be tough, they should know that there are times to just rub some dirt on the wound and get back into the action. That sort of language doesn't bother me one bit.

What does bother me though is when men refuse to acknowledge pain at all, and refuse to acknowledge what they are going through, which in a twisted irony, leads directly to more suffering.

In other words, as a man, yes sometimes you do just grab some mud to cover the wound and get back into the fight. However, too often that becomes the default for men, for all forms of pain, all the time.

Acknowledge the pain, it is real. Don't bother pretending there is no pain in your life, and that everything is all Sunshine, Rainbows, and Unicorns. You might fool a few people who don't know you, for a little while anyway. However, you'll eventually be pulled down into the pit of suffering.

Become aware of what you say to yourself, when you are in pain. Become aware of the stories you are telling yourself and what the annoying voice is saying to you. Become an active player in your life; make the conscious choice as to how you are going to react to the situations you find yourself in.

That recognition is where the change happens. Once you start paying attention to what you are saying to yourself, and how you are reacting to situations, you can then start to make the choice to react differently.

Does this change overnight? Not a chance. However, you do need to know that it is very possible. It is possible for you to go through life without the level of suffering you have now.

Will you have pain, in your life? Absolutely.

Will you suffer because of that pain? Only if you choose to do so.

Fifty-Five
THE SUPERSTITION OF SECURITY

I mentioned earlier that, as men, we need adventure. We need something to push us, to challenge us, and to drive us forward to new places. When we don't have this, when we don't have any adventure, we slowly die on the inside, often becoming bored and disinterested in the world and our place in it.

On the opposite side of adventure is safety and security. The security and safety of a paycheck, of an income, and of trying to ensure that tomorrow will be the same as today.

The difficult thing is that in order to get safety and security we usually have to give up on adventure. This makes sense to us at a definitional level; after all, how can we go out on some grand adventure while still being safe and secure at the same time? The simple answer is that we cannot.

Is there risk in our lives when we have security? Are we really safe and secure if we have eliminated risk and eliminated adventure?

Our society often assumes that if we have security we have therefore reduced risk, and in some instances that might be true. However, there is a flipside, there is another viewpoint on this issue, and that is, what risks might we be increasing in men when we move towards security?

Do we increase the risk in men that they will disengage with their children? Do we increase the risk in men that they will disengage with their wives? Do we increase the risk in men that they will disengage with society and life in general?

I'd argue that the overwhelming evidence is showing that yes, that is exactly what is happening, and that those risks are becoming reality. More and more men, day after day, are disengaging with their own lives. They are retreating into the comfort and safety of familiar, safe, and secure places.

Men are retreating into the safety and security of their TVs and video games. Men are retreating into the safety and security of their computers, mobile phones, and online worlds.

Men are retreating from the hard conversations with their wives. Men are retreating from the duty of raising their children. Men are retreating from the responsibility to lead their families. Men are retreating from the opportunity to connect with God.

They are retreating into their safe and secure places, but is that somehow better for men and their families? Is that better for our society? Is that not a somber and serious risk?

Those are the hard questions we have to look at and questions we have to come to grips with. I know that when I see a man who has chosen the safety and security of disengagement that this is the same man who will not have adventure in his life.

Beyond the serious issue of a man disengaging with the world around him, are there other risks when he chooses security and safety over adventure?

Again, I would suggest absolutely, yes.

Why is it that so many men die within such a short time from their retirement? Why is it that men are willing to commit suicide over changes in their lives that disrupt the security their paycheck provided?

Author David P. Goldman wrote about the volume of suicides that took place in a short few years at France Telecom. Here are two key quotes from his article:

"… the mortal sin that motivated two dozen suicides in 2009 at France Telecom, the dullest place in the habitable world, where people go to do nothing and make a living at it. Twenty–four employees at the French monopoly killed themselves in the past 18 months, and another 13 have attempted suicide."

"…the global economic crisis has shaken the foundations of state finances in Europe, and bloated entities such as France Telecom must adjust. A consistent pattern informs the suicide notes of France Telecom workers: the fear of downsizing, demotion, and reassignment is too much for them to bear. The desire for security is an addiction: the more security one obtains, the less secure one feels."

The last part of that quote is key; the more security one obtains, the less secure one feels. That might seem like a contradiction, but it isn't.

As men, there is almost an instinctive understanding of those lines, even without taking the time to dig deep on them and dissect the meanings. We know that we need adventure, we know this in our guts, even if we don't know how to articulate that need.

We also know that once we become disengaged and addicted to security, something inside dies. The addiction to safety and security becomes strong, like all other addictions. If we then find that addiction is in danger, then the drastic measure of suicide suddenly seems an option. Men would rather leave the world than have their illusion of safety and security destroyed.

A primary reason for suicide in men is that they are not providing enough for their family and that they feel useless and worthless; that they can be replaced if the security the paycheck provides is gone. Safe and secure can directly lead to feelings of worthlessness and being useless. Yes, I would consider that a very serious risk.

We have to recognize these issues. We have to be willing to look at the reality of what happens in our lives, what happens to us, as men, if we start down the path of safety and security.

When we make that choice, when we trade in our adventure for security, a small piece of us is dying, or at the very minimum is going to hibernate, possibly never to wake up again. When we make that choice, when we try to eliminate risk in exchange for safety, another small piece dies or hibernates.

Over time, we end up with an entire society of confused, disengaged, and hibernating men.

Yet the world wonders, "Where have all the men gone?"

To which I answer, they are all around us. Only they have no adventure, they have no risk, they have nothing that pushes or compels them to anything more than safe, secure, and small lives.

It's time that we, as men, wake up to this reality. It is time we engage with life, it is time we take some risks, have some adventure, and return to being the men that God created us to be.

I'll end this chapter, with a wonderful quote from Helen Keller. I suggest you really take some time to think about this one. She said, "Security is mostly a superstition. It does not exist in nature, nor do the children of men as a whole experience it. Avoiding danger is no safer in the long run than outright exposure. Life is either a daring adventure or nothing."

Fifty-Six
LEADING YOUR CHILDREN

*T*here is a big, as in major, problem in our society. This cuts both ways, meaning it applies to men and women, although it does so in different ways.

- The problem is that far too many men and women do not understand their role as a parent. Let me cut to the chase here, right at the start of this chapter:
- Your children are not supposed to have the job of making you happy.
- Your children are not props to use.
- Your children are not supposed to look to you as their best friend.
- Your children are not to validate your past.
- Your children are not to fulfill your dreams.

I could keep building the list, but I think you have a high–level idea of where I'm going with this. These lines seem clearly to go against what society often says and what so many do. As a significant man however, you're not willing to blindly follow what others do and you are willing to do the right thing.

The first line, and this is often more towards mothers than fathers, is that your kids are not supposed to have the job of making you happy. Over time, this becomes an enormous burden on your children, a constant pressure, and they will feel that weight their entire lives.

If you transfer your happiness to anyone, that is bad, but when you do it to your children, it is harmful. They will feel that duty forever, a duty that is impossible to maintain. To transfer the responsibility for your happiness to your children can be very harmful to them, and can end up creating lasting resentment (especially later in life when they start to investigate their own journeys, as adults).

The point is this: Your happiness is your choice, it is your responsibility, and it is up to you. Never put that burden onto your children.

The second line, about your children not being props, is an issue amplified due to social media. Far too often parents are using their kids in this way, posing them for the perfect pictures, sharing the perfect articles, openly using them to show how great the parent is, with little regard for how the child is going to be impacted by being used in that regard. Photos and posts with kids as props is all about the parent, that is using children, and doing so in an unhealthy manner.

Now the third line, about being the best friend of your child. This one often strikes a nerve, and requires explanation.

Your job, as a father, is to be a father first. First and always, you are the father of your children. A parent makes very different decisions than a friend. A parent has a very different perspective than a friend.

Your children need to you to lead, to make decisions, to discipline, and to set boundaries, while they also need you to play, to talk, to listen, to have fun, and to laugh. They always need to know you are their father first. After being their father, then the friendship comes. Your children need their own friends, their own relationships, their own places to confide in, and their own circle of influence.

You need to be a safe harbor for your kids, and you do need to be a friend to your kids, but that comes after you have made decisions and led your children as a father.

Over time, as your children grow older, the friendship element grows, until you have nearly a peer level relationship, though you never are exactly a peer. Just remember that you will always be their father first, even when your children have children of their own.

To keep moving, and obviously each of these points is a lengthy conversation, the next line about your children is that they are not to validate your past. You can think about this point in combination with the next line about how your children are not there to fulfill your dreams.

This happens more with men than it does with women, where men look to the achievements and abilities of their children in order to validate their own past and to fulfill their own dreams.

Most often, for men, this is the case in regards to sports. When men look for their children (this tends to happen more with sons than with daughters, but is starting to happen with daughters more frequently) to live out their hopes and dreams, it generally does not end well.

These men look to the successes of their children as validation of themselves as fathers. If the child does well in the sport, the father equates that to him doing well as a dad. Every practice has to be perfect, every game has to be a victory, and every shot has to be made.

The constant pressure on the child to perform becomes overwhelming, with little to no time left over for the child to actually be a child. Over time, this can build into actual contempt for the sport/activity and create a gulf between the father and the child, and worse, it can create contempt between them. It becomes very easy for the sport to become something that the child starts to dislike, even if they are good at it.

One of the most famous examples of this comes from Andre Agassi, who shared his experience in his autobiography. He shared two key points that fathers need to understand. They are:

"I play tennis for a living even though I hate tennis, hate it with a dark and secret passion and always have."

"I know for myself—it's something you've done since you were six years old, and there's a sense that if you stop giving 100% you are doomed to failure, and that is unacceptable. No wonder so many players hate their sport—the surprise is that so few admit it."

That last line, about how so many players hate their sport but won't admit it is a major point to take in. I'm willing to bet that the biggest reason so few will admit it is due to the reaction of their fathers and others who have placed the burden of performance on the shoulders of the players. The children do not want to let their fathers down, and do want to live up to the expectations.

To continue with this, during an interview after his book came out, Andre was asked to elaborate on his comments, did he really hate tennis? All fathers need to hear what he said. He said this:

"It's more like a hate–love relationship, you know? Tennis was something I certainly didn't choose, I didn't choose it as a young man. My father kind of pushed it on me. I felt fear to not do it, not in any sort of form of abuse, but in the form of just having the pressure of the world on my shoulders. He introduced me as "The Future #1 Player in the World" and then I went to an academy that I hated. It was more like a glorified prison camp and my only way out of there was to succeed, and I succeeded and found myself on the world stage."

Now not every father puts the pressure on his child the way that Agassi's father did. But, too many do, most of whom don't realize it when they are doing it. The pressure isn't always obvious, in fact it is usually entirely overlooked during the game. Too often, the fathers are lost in the glory of their child's performance, and become entirely oblivious to the fact that their own son or daughter is miserable and feels like there are in a glorified prison camp, and the only way out is to succeed.

Jokes by the father about how his son is going to buy his parents a house and Ferrari once he "goes pro" are not the kind of jokes that children forget.

Too many fathers are running around thinking they were only one shot away from the big leagues, and now their own children can carry out their broken dream. Just spend five minutes at any sports event for kids; you can see these dads all over the sidelines and in the bleachers.

Your children are not to validate your past, and they are not to carry out your dreams. You need to let that go. You need to understand that no matter what your son or daughter does, you have to remove any burden that you might have given them, accidentally or on purpose, about them fulfilling your dreams.

Your job is to help shape your children into great adults, into young men and women who are working hard to be good people themselves. Your job isn't to ensure they have any specific career, any specific hobby, or any specific interest. Your job is to lead your children, set an example for them, teach them, and love them.

Your sons will learn what kind of man to become from the example you set. Your sons will learn how to treat a woman, based on your example. Your daughters will learn what kind of man to marry from the example you set. Your daughters will learn how they should be treated by a man, based on your example.

Your kids might have no interest in the family business, so don't make them. Your kids might have no interest in the sport you loved, so don't force them. Your kids might have interests and loves that you do not even understand, so do accept them.

Your kids will have their own hopes, their own dreams, their own goals, their own passions, and their own purpose in this world. Do all you can to teach them and to lead them in growing up into good adults, adults who are following their own dreams on their own paths.

I'll leave you with this verse to consider: "Fathers, do not exasperate your children; instead, bring them up in the training and instruction of the Lord." (Ephesians 6:4)

Fifty-Seven
RELEASE HER

*I*f you've been around for a few years, you have probably heard this famous saying:

"Women get married hoping they can change their man, while men get married hoping their woman never changes."

What happens when that phrase becomes more than a saying, when it becomes the reality of the life you find yourself living? How do you deal with that?

When you start to see the entire world differently from your wife, what happens? What happens when you see that the lawn needs to be mowed and you figure out when you will do it, in the next week or so… while she sees that the lawn needs to be moved and thinks that, if you loved her, you would have already done it?

Do you start to wonder when she is going to change back into the loving woman you fell in love with? Do you wonder where that woman went?

Do you realize that, at the same time, she is wondering when you are going to change into the man who gets her, who understands her, and who will take care of what she wants, without her asking you to do it?

This is a problem, obviously, and for many that is an understatement. If I were to guess, I would say that nearly all relationships run into this problem one point or another.

What it all boils down to, at the core, are unspoken expectations. Both you and she have created rules and expectations in your heads about what the other person is supposed to be doing. And now you are expecting her, and she is expecting you, to act in accordance to those rules that she (and you) never even knew existed.

You think something is trivial and you'll get to it later. She thinks that you are showing that you are irresponsible and that you do not love her.

Your eyes catch a beautiful woman for a second, and you forget about it within minutes. She sees that and thinks you no longer love her, that you are now comparing her against that other woman, and that she will never live up to the other woman.

There is this core misunderstanding, and this core problem of unspoken expectations.

She wants you to change to meet her expectations. You want her to change to meet your expectations.

So what is a man to do?

You might turn into trying mode. This is where you try everything. You try to cut the grass early, you try to do some more dishes, and you try to do more stuff around the house. Yet it seems that nothing works.

She still seems closed off to you, still questioning you, now she might be questioning your motives and your reasons.

In your head you're thinking, who cares what my reasons are, isn't it enough that I'm actually doing these things?

This then goes back to the core expectations. It will take time for her. She might be thinking, is he just doing these things because he doesn't want me upset, or is he doing them because he really loves me and is going to do these things for me.

At this point, most men throw up their hands in confusion and frustration. For men, if you do the thing, it is done, the reason why isn't even on your list. For women, the reason why the you do the thing is a primary item on her list.

This is one of those times when us men are speaking a completely different language from the women in our lives. So stop trying to figure it out for now.

You cannot make someone else change. Ever. You might be able to force some temporary changes, but those often lead to resentment or built up anger, so that isn't a good idea anyway. What you can do, is to lead. You can set the example. You can sit in the driver's seat and take control of the wheel.

You can release her from the burden that you have placed on her, a burden you likely have not realized you've given her. Many of the men I speak with have never stepped back to see this burden. It is big. It is heavy. It is one she never asked to carry. Yet you placed it squarely on her shoulders.

You can take charge of your situation. You can stop blaming her. You can stop trying to get her to change. You can stop using that as an excuse for why you have not yet done what you know you should.

Step up, take action, and lead your family. Release her from that pressure.

If you have children, let them see your example of how a husband should be. Let them see that you have made the choice, for you and how you are going to live, to take care of your family. Let them see how you choose to act around your wife. Let them see how you choose to talk with your wife.

If you decide to do this, (and you should), you might decide to tell her what you are doing. However, do not expect anything to change when you tell her. In fact, it might get worse for a while when you tell her.

Because, she has heard it before. Possibly with your words, but more likely with your actions. She doesn't want to hear it anymore. She wants to see it, and more than once or for a short time.

You have to be ready for the challenges that will come up during this time of transition.

She is going to wonder why you are doing it, as I mentioned above. She is going to wonder how long it will last. She might even be suspicious as to what you are actually doing.

That's ok. Your actions and decisions, over the years, led to this place.

Do not expect a few weeks to erase all of the past. If this is your real choice, if this is what you are choosing to do, you can expect it to take time.

This leads us back to expectations. There is a conversation you need to have with her, and guys this one might really be hard for you to have. However, if you are one of the guys who is working on becoming a significant man, then this conversation has to take place. It has to.

Ok, deep breath.

You need to get those unspoken expectations out in the open. You need to know what she has been holding inside, all the expectations she has about what you should and should not be doing, in general, and all the expectations about how you should and should not be leading as a husband and father.

You have to listen. You cannot judge here. You cannot complain here. You cannot discount here. You cannot tell her why she is wrong here. You cannot defend yourself here. You cannot do any of that.

Use your logical brain here. Really listen. She is telling you her inner secrets, respect that. She is telling you the root causes she sees, respect that.

If you use your logic, and you are actually listening, you can get to the core issues that have been causing so much stress, so much discontent, and possibly even the reasons for the outright anger and fighting, if it has come to that.

Again, do not argue here, do not judge, do not complain, and do not defend; do none of that. Not even a small tiny bit. Hold your tongue and listen, and even take notes if you need to.

When she has finished, and let her talk for as long as she wants, thank her. Give her a kiss and a hug. Let her know that you have listened, and you have really heard, what she has told you.

For the third time, do not argue and get defensive, just listen. I cannot emphasize how important that really is. Cross that line here, and it is likely that you are never going to have this conversation again, ever. (Remember how you can retreat into your fortress? Well, guess what? She has a fortress too, and you might not be invited inside!)

Now what you are not going to do is simply nod and say "yes dear" or whatever equivalent you personally use. She is smart enough to know that means you are not really listening, and she will shut down.

You also are not going to simply rattle off and jump right into saying that you will start doing what she has mentioned. With the history you have together, she is not going to believe you. You know you're not going to be able to hold to every single thing right away anyway, so don't start this new phase with a lie.

Instead, you are taking internal notes (again, write them down if you have to) of everything that she has held inside for all these years. You might be surprised at just how simple some of these issues will be for you to take care of, but you didn't even know they existed. There could be a handful of issues you can address that are minor, in your mind, but major to her—and you can easily get to work on them.

That is the reality of most relationships. You want to please her anyway. You are happy to do these things, but you are not a mind reader. She might think you should be. OK, that is the reality, don't fight it, deal with it.

If you are one of the guys who is able to have this conversation, she is doing what all guys want—she is telling you what issues exist. That's it! Now you have what you have always wanted, you have a map, a set of plans to follow. The expectations are out in the open. You've wanted the guide book to follow your entire relationship, and she just gave you one customized to her exact needs.

Because at the end of the day, you cannot change her. Just as she cannot change you. As mentioned earlier, you could somehow force some temporary changes on one another, but that will not end well. One, or more likely both, of you will hold that as a negative and resentment, which is a killer of relationships.

Your job here is to step up and lead. Your job here is for you to take control of your life, and for you to make the choice about what you can control and change. Your job here is to release her from the burden you have placed on her shoulders.

You make changes all the time, we all do. The saying that people do not change is a myth. You changed when you started your business, when you got your job, when you got promoted, when you got laid off… you are changing all the time.

In this case, you are in control of your changes. You are not changing her; you are changing you. This is a big one guys, take some time to really let it sink in. And, no pun intended:

Do this and you might just find your life and relationship, changing into something amazing.

Fifty-Eight
EXPAND YOUR VISION

In this life, one thing I know for sure, from working with so many men over the years, is that the vision you have for yourself and the vision you have for your life have a direct impact on the life you actually live.

Your vision, meaning the image and expectation that you have of your life now and will have in the future, is almost always the exact life that you are living now and the life that you will be living in the future.

Your vision about your marriage affects the reality of your marriage. Your vision about your income affects the reality of your income. Your vision about being a father affects the reality of how you function as a father. Your vision about your health affects the reality of your fitness level and health level. And on and on… in every aspect of your life your vision affects your reality.

And whatever that vision is, good, bad, or indifferent, that is the life you are living. It is rarely the case that your vision and your reality are completely opposite. You have already brought your vision to life, likely without even realizing it.

So let me ask you this: if you were working with me, and I asked you to articulate and describe your specific vision of your life, as it is right now, what would you say?

If I asked you to articulate and describe your vision for exactly what your life will be like in six months, one year, and three years from now, what would you say?

I'm not asking about what you hope for; I'm not asking about what you think would be nice to maybe have in your life someday. I'm asking you to accurately describe what you see in your future and precisely how you are going to get there (remember the Battle Plan chapter?).

Here is the truth guys: the vast majority of men don't even have a real vision of their lives today, let alone a vision of what their lives will be like a year from now. So don't feel bad if you don't either, that is where most men are right now.

The majority of men have no vision of what they want their marriage to be like, no vision of what they want their finances to look like, no vision of what their parenting will become, no vision of what it is like to be connected to God, really they have no vision at all. They are simply floating down the river of life, taking each day as it comes, and not steering themselves, or their family, in any direction.

These men will often say they want their marriage to be solid, that they want their finances to be strong, that they want to be rich, that they want to be a great Dad, and that they want to experience what that connection to God is like, but that is as far as the vision goes. They have a vague hope and then nothing beyond saying that they want those things.

If you've never thought about this before I can accept having no vision, up to today in your life, but that can't continue as you move forward. Not only do you need to have a vision for the core areas of your life, but you have to expand and grow that vision to be much, much bigger.

God wants more for you. Just like you don't want to see your own children struggle and live small lives, never using their talents and never following their dreams, neither does He want to see you struggle and live a small life. He wants you to want more out of your own life. He wants you to want to expand your own vision of what your life can, and should, be like.

Before you can expand your vision into something more, there are some things you need to understand:

- If your vision is to remain small, to remain broke, to remain unhealthy, to remain where you are, then that is exactly what you will make sure happens.
- If your vision is that you just barely make it from one paycheck to the next, then that is what will happen in your life.
- If your vision is that you won't really be a great father, that you won't ever lead your children the way you think you can, then that is exactly what you will make sure happens.
- If your vision is that you will fight with your wife, and that she doesn't understand you, then guess what? Yes, that is exactly what you will make happen.

Are you seeing a pattern here yet? The truth is that your brain will work overtime to make sure that your vision comes true, no matter if that is a big vision or a small one, no matter if that is a positive vision or a negative one, that is what your reality will be.

You will work hard, consciously and subconsciously to bring your visions to reality. You will find that luck and coincidence (whether you consider them good or bad) always seems to line up with the vision you have for your life. A man who tells himself that he always has bad luck seems to… always have bad luck. A man who tells himself that he always finds himself with unfortunate coincidence seems to… always find those unfortunate coincidences.

Until you grow your vision into more, you will continue to get exactly what you are currently getting. Do not be surprised when nothing changes, if your vision for your life doesn't change.

Show me a man who has no vision for what this year will be, and I know that this year will end up just about the same as last year. His income will end about the same. His fitness will end about the same. His marriage will end about the same. His life next year will pretty much be just what it was this year.

What this means is that you must do the work and create a clear vision for your life. You must have a clear vision about your marriage, you must have a clear vision about your fitness level, you must have a clear vision about your financial health, you must have a clear vision about your spiritual connection, and you must have a clear vision about how you will lead as a father.

When you are creating your vision, be specific. Be exact. Create a precise and clear vision. Don't say, I hope to be healthy next year. That's weak and won't help you at all. Instead, say, I am 30 pounds lighter, I exercise 30 minutes every day, and I love who I have become. That's more powerful and effective.

Create a similar vision, precise and specific, about every aspect of your life. And make it big! Don't hold back here. Make it a vision of the life you truly want to live.

Expand your vision into greater things. Do not settle for what you have now, and be open to the understanding that it is ok for you to want more and it is ok for you to want to become the significant man that you know you can become.

Before wrapping up this chapter, I want to quickly add that vision alone isn't enough. You can think about increasing your income all you want, but until you act, you won't grow rich. Throughout this book there has been a theme of acting on your choices. You actually have to do the work.

The vision is so you know what you expect and where you are going. The action is what will get you there; you have to act upon what you are learning.

It is time to expect more. It is time to be ok with wanting more. It is time to expand your vision.

Fifty-Nine

WHAT IS YOUR LEGACY?

By now, you know that I like questions. I like asking them, thinking about them, and working through their answers. And you know that I like real, deep, and significant questions. If you and I ever spend time together, don't expect me to spend much time asking you about the weather or about last night's big game. Expect me to ask questions that go right into the core of being a man and navigating through this life we are all living together.

One of those significant questions is this: What is your legacy?

When you die, when you have left this world, what exactly will your legacy be? Will you be gone and forgotten in a short time? Will you have created something that lasts beyond your death?

In the simple dictionary terms, the definition of the word legacy is: *(Noun) An amount of money or property left to someone in a will.*

How bland, boring, and uninspiring. I am not a fan of that description. For many reasons, but let's start with the obvious.

That sort of definition is stating that if you don't have money or property to leave in a will, then you don't have a legacy. That is 100% untrue. Legacy goes far beyond money and property.

Before moving to those other points though, I want to make clear that leaving behind money and property for others is a good thing, there is nothing wrong with having that as a goal in your life and having a specific plan of action for getting there. If you choose to leave each of your children and grandchildren a million dollars, then get to work and make that happen.

However, the issues that extend beyond property and money are where you build a real legacy. That is where I want to focus this chapter here; the real part of your legacy, the part that will matter the most at the end of your life.

To have a legacy that lasts, a legacy that goes beyond your money and things, you need to impact people at a deeper level. You need to have made an impression on people, deep in their souls, which goes further than those surface issues of wealth and expensive toys.

You shape your legacy by how you live your life, not by the stuff you leave around after it ends. You build your legacy on purpose or others will build it by default. Either way, you will have a legacy.

The question is, what will that legacy be? Is that legacy going to be one that lives long, having an impact on generations after you've died, or is that legacy going to be short, fading away into the shadows and the busyness of life?

The awesome news is that you have great control over the answer to that question. You are the one who has the single greatest impact on deciding what your legacy is going to be.

As you continue on your journey, you become the man in charge of your life; you are in control of the direction you take. Since that is the case, we should be looking at the ways of building a legacy with purpose, the ways of creating a legacy that lasts beyond your death. So let's look at what some of those things are, and look at some of the things you can start doing, today, to build your legacy.

Your legacy will start with your children and with the people that you have a direct influence on today in the example you set for them. If you don't have children, then your focus is clearly on all the other people you are impacting and how you are living your life. However, if you do have children, your legacy focus needs to be there first.

Who you are as a man, as a husband, as a father, how you live your life, the examples that you are setting, the impression you give people, the influence that you have on others, and on and on.... those are the elements of your legacy that live much longer than money and property.

When you think about all the various chapters you have read in this book, I hope you can see now that they are all part of you intentionally building your legacy. Every chapter works together towards you living that significant life you want to live, which also happens to be part of the battle plan for how you create a powerful legacy that lasts through time.

I know many guys like to have a list of specific "do this" ideas, so here is a list for you:

- Create a powerful mission and vision for your life. Know what it is you want and get to work making that happen. Take control of your direction, become the captain of your own ship.

- Learn to really listen and engage with your wife. Fulfill your covenant to be a husband, and keep growing in your relationship with your wife. Love her every day, and make a conscious choice to work on becoming a better man and better husband all the time.

- Lead your children. You are their father first; own that role with pride and do that job with as much energy as any other job you ever do. Lead them as a father and a man and teach them how to grow up into good adults themselves.

- Own your current reality. No matter if you are in a good place, or a bad place, own that reality. Take charge and refuse to blame anyone else anymore. Never allow yourself to fall into the victim mindset and mentality.

- Extend your life beyond yourself. Look for, and create, opportunities for you to affect and lead other people, and build up something beyond you and your own needs and desires.

- Be a man of action, executing your battle plan. When you learn something, put it into practice. When you need to learn something, be open to finding a solution. Do the work you need to do, and keep taking action.

If you do this, if you become a man who leads his family, who loves his wife, who has a life with a mission and a vision, who owns his reality, who is creating opportunities to build and affect people all around him, and who is a man of action… you will absolutely have built a legacy that lives on.

That is the life of a significant man… and it is yours for the taking.

Sixty
WHAT'S NEXT?

onclusions to books like this are always interesting. You can have a
simple summary, maybe a set of related quotes, or even a simple thank
you. I have something a bit different in mind.

To begin, yes I do thank you for reading all of this. I've often been told
that men don't really want to read and that they don't really want to read
anything that is deep or that questions the status quo. I don't believe that, and
I've seen it personally in the men I work with. In fact, I think the majority of
men want to get to that level, and just haven't had a good means of getting
there. So thank you for reading to the end here, and thank you for being
the kind of man who wants more out of life and is willing to consider new
questions and ideas.

What I would like to leave you with is a plan of action, something to
combine with the list in the prior chapter about your legacy. These two chapters
should become part of your battle plan. I'm leaving you with next steps for you
to use, starting today, in your own journey towards becoming an even more
significant man.

1. Start applying all that you learned in this book. Be willing to go deep with all the questions, look for the answers that will guide you as you go forward. Be willing to do the work you need to do.
2. Start becoming closer to your wife. Learn to really listen to her, learn to connect with her, and learn to have a powerful relationship with her. Become the husband she desires.
3. Start becoming the leader your kids need. Kids need fathers. Don't just be there to play and buy things, really be a father. Teach them. Lead them. Love them. Become the father they deserve.
4. Start connecting more with God. Take the time to read something, watch something, or listen to something every day that can expand your understanding and your connection with Him. There is incredible peace and power in developing and growing that connection.
5. Start building your life towards something greater than you; build something greater than the stuff and the toys. As discussed in the last chapter, you get to build your legacy; there is no reason you can't start that today.

Imagine your life, one year from right now, if you started taking action today—and then imagine your life, one year from right now, if you waited another year before starting anything discussed in this book. Which one of those lives do you want to live? As always, the choice is yours.

It is time for you to start becoming the significant man that God created you to be!

SIGNIFICANT MAN LIVE

This book is the beginning of your journey, not the end. It is where the next level of your life can start, as long as you refuse to stay where you are and you choose to take action. If you apply even one of the ideas contained in this book, it will have been worth your investment in these pages.

For men who want to go beyond this book, who want to push towards faster results, who want to wake up, and who want to empower their lives, there is the Significant Man Live experience.

Significant Man Live is three days of intense mentoring and training in the key areas of life that lead to the biggest changes in men who are ready for more.

If you want to learn how to live the life you were created to live, if you want to see changes in your business, if you want to become the hero, the warrior, and the leader you were created to be, then you have to be open to something you may have never considered before.

If you are willing to do the work, if you are willing to take action, if you are willing to take a stand for you and your future, then Significant Man Live might be for you.

If you're feeling the call, if you know it is time for you to do this, then please do head over to www.SignificantMan.com, and see if what we offer is the right fit for you.

As always, the choice is yours. You can continue on your current path, you can find another way forward, or you can join the other powerful men who are called to experience Significant Man Live. Regardless of what you choose, you will get exactly what is right for you, so you can't go wrong.

Significant Man Crest

FURTHER READING

I've been influenced by many authors over the years, and you can see their influence all throughout this book. The following are all books that have shaped me, and I highly recommend that you read them along your journey:

Gordon Dalbey, *"Healing the Masculine Soul"*
Stu Weber, *"Tender Warrior"*
John Eldredge, *"Wild at Heart"*
CS Lewis, *"Mere Christianity"*
Max Lucado, *"Fearless"*
Bob P. Buford, *"Game Plan"*
Gay Hendricks, *"The Big Leap"*
Viktor Frankl, *"Man's Search for Meaning"*
Shaunti Feldhahn, *"For Men Only"*
Dr. Emerson Eggerichs, *"Love and Respect"*
Dennis Prager, *"Happiness is a Serious Problem"*

Additional writers and philosophers I strongly suggest you spend time reading: Marcus Aurelius, Epictetus, Seneca, Hierocles, Rufus, Plato, Socrates, Aristotle, and other classics from days gone by. Be open to expanding your mind in ways you might never have considered.

BIBLE VERSES FOR MEN

"In everything set them an example by doing what is good. In your teaching show integrity, seriousness, and soundness of speech that cannot be condemned, so that those who oppose you may be ashamed because they have nothing bad to say about us." Titus 2:7–8 (NIV)

The above is my personal cornerstone verse for the work I do with Significant Man. The following verses, from the English Standard Version of the Bible, have spoken to me over the years, and I pray they may do the same for you:

"As iron sharpens iron, so one man sharpens another." Proverbs 27:17

"Blessed is the man who remains steadfast under trial, for when he has stood the test he will receive the crown of life, which God has promised to those who love Him." James 1:12

"Be watchful. Stand firm in the faith. Act like men. Be Strong. Let all that you do, be done in love." 1 Corinthians 16:13–14

"Husbands, love your wives as Christ loved the church and gave himself up for her." Ephesians 5:25

"Do you see a man skillful in his work? He will stand before kings: he will not stand before obscure men." Proverbs 22:29

"Besides this you know the time, that the hour has come for you to wake from sleep. For salvation is nearer to us now than when we first believed. This night is far and gone; the day is at hand. So then let us cast off the works of darkness and put on the armor of light." Romans 13:11–12

"I have fought the good fight, I have finished the race, I have kept the faith. Henceforth, there is laid up for me the crown of righteousness, which the Lord, the righteous judge, will award to me on that Day, and not only to me but also to all who have loved his appearing." 2 Timothy 4:7–8

"For though we walk in the flesh, we are not waging war according to the flesh. For the weapons of our warfare are not of the flesh but have divine power to destroy strongholds." 2 Corinthians 10:3–4

"Blessed by the Lord, my rock, who trains my hands for war, and my fingers for battle; He is my steadfast love and my fortress, my stronghold and my deliverer, my shield and He in whom I take refuge, who subdues peoples under me." Psalm 144:1–2

"Finally, be strong in the Lord and in the strength of his might. Put on the whole armor of God, that you may be able to stand against the schemes of the devil. For we do not wrestle against flesh and blood, but against the rulers, against the authorities, against the cosmic powers over this present darkness, against the spiritual forces of evil in the heavenly places. Therefore, take up the whole armor of God, that you may be able to withstand in the evil day, and having done all, to stand firm." Ephesians 6:10–13

ABOUT THE AUTHOR

After the painful loss of his home, business, income, life savings, and even his own identity as a man, Warren Peterson determined to use his experience and calling to help others.

He founded Significant Man, an organization focused on leading men towards becoming the heroes, warriors, and leaders they were created to be. He loves teaching and mentoring men, seeing the changes in their lives, and the positive results in their families.

Warren lives in beautiful Colorado with his wife and their four children.

To learn more about his work, please visit him online at:
www.SignificantMan.com

If *Becoming a Significant Man* has had an impact on you, please email your personal story to Warren: Story@SignificantMan.com

A free eBook edition is available with the purchase of this book.

To claim your free eBook edition:

1. Download the Shelfie app.
2. Write your name in upper case in the box.
3. Use the Shelfie app to submit a photo.
4. Download your eBook to any device.

Shelfie

A free eBook edition is available
with the purchase of this print book.

CLEARLY PRINT YOUR NAME ABOVE IN UPPER CASE

Instructions to claim your free eBook edition:
1. Download the Shelfie app for Android or iOS
2. Write your name in **UPPER CASE** above
3. Use the Shelfie app to submit a photo
4. Download your eBook to any device

Print & Digital Together Forever.

Snap a photo

Free eBook

Read anywhere

We connect Morgan James published
authors with live and online events
and audiences whom will benefit
from their expertise.